Praise for Ignite

'This is a great gift to our churches and communities today. Patrick and Debbie's passion and experience shine through in this inspiring and practical step-by-step guide to Ignite, and how to build relational and lasting community, through a new and innovative approach to church. This book is a hugely valuable resource.'
The Revd Jonathon Arnold, executive director of The Social Justice Network, Diocese of Canterbury

'Born in one of the most derived parishes in England, Ignite is much more than a way of doing outreach. People who would not normally come near a church – who might feel themselves to be imposters, even – are often adamant that this is their church. Patrick and Debbie Ellisdon are the practitioners and visionaries who brought Ignite to birth. You will hear their down-to-earth and gentle voices through this book. Ignite is now planted and contextualised in various places around the Diocese of Canterbury, but all of them carry the essential Ignite DNA – a way of being church when "church ways" have sometimes got in the way, so that people who often assume they have no place know that they belong.'
Steve Coneys, mission and growth adviser, Diocese of Canterbury

'This book is a wonderful testimony of how God can shape a church to minister to those around us; to reveal the love of Jesus to those we often fail to connect with. This book not only tells the story of Ignite but also its thinking, theology and process with lots of wonderful resources to use to share the gospel.'
The Revd Mike Resch, vicar of St Marks in Harrogate and part of the New Wine Leadership Community

'This book is for our time. When I was archdeacon in Canterbury Diocese, I was on many an occasion moved to tears by the testimonies of those who have come to faith through Ignite services, as outlined in this book.'
The Revd Stephen Taylor, vicar of St Marys Battersea

'Ignite is not just a study guide as to how to make new Christians; it is the lived experience of those whose lives have been touched by the good news of Jesus Christ – touched through the hospitality of a welcoming community whose members have been willing to share their own experiences of meeting Jesus. The church owes a huge debt of gratitude to Patrick and Debbie Ellisdon, whose passion to share Jesus is evident on every page of this book.'
The Rt Revd Trevor Wilmott, bishop for the Channel Islands and former Bishop of Dover

Ign*te

The Gospel in Action

How to share faith, build community and do church, differently

Patrick and Debbie Ellisdon

BRF
Ministries

BRF Ministries

15 The Chambers, Vineyard
Abingdon OX14 3FE
+44 (0)1865 319700 | brf.org.uk

Bible Reading Fellowship (BRF) is a charity (233280) and company limited by guarantee
(301324), registered in England and Wales

EU Authorised Representative: Easy Access System Europe –
Mustamäe tee 50, 10621 Tallinn, Estonia, **gpsr.requests@easproject.com**

ISBN 978 1 80039 301 1
First published 2025
10 9 8 7 6 5 4 3 2 1 0
All rights reserved

CONTENTS

PART III   PRACTICALITIES

PART IV   THE STORY

Foreword

Jesus got in trouble with the religious leaders of his day for making a beeline for those whom they did not consider to be respectable. He hung out with people on the edges of society, those who did not easily fit into organised religion or the social pecking order. Outrageously (according to the religious leaders), he ate with them, which in Middle Eastern culture expresses deep fellowship and friendship. Jesus saw no societal barrier to the people that he loved, taught, healed and prayed with. We can imagine that he cried, laughed and danced with them too. He was their friend, and he is also our friend.

In the Church of England, we have not always been very good at following Jesus' example in this respect. Let's face it, we are all more comfortable around people who are similar to us. But as Jesus' followers we have been commissioned to share the good news of Jesus Christ with everyone!

The Ignite model was born in the diocese of Canterbury by Patrick and Debbie Ellisdon with the simple passion and desire to share the good news with those that the church rarely reaches out to in an intentional way. In this book you will find a tried-and-tested, step-by-step guide on how to get started in your community. My four priorities (for the diocese of Canterbury) are prayer, study of the scripture, evangelism and generosity. Ignite models all of these in a fresh and exciting way.

I hope you will be blessed and encouraged as you read these pages. More importantly, my prayer is that you will be inspired to step out of your comfort zone, and in so doing take the good news to those who are marginalised in our communities, thus creating a space where they can get to know Jesus. I pray for strength for you as you work through the inevitable challenges this may involve. I pray you will 'come home rejoicing' with stories of new friendships made. And finally, I pray that you too are blessed as you help expand the kingdom where you are.

+ Rose

The Rt Revd Rose Hudson-Wilkin, Bishop of Dover

Introduction

Well done for at least opening this book and peeking inside! We are guessing that – like us – you probably love Jesus and would really like to help other people get to know him as well. If so, then you are in the right place. Nowadays, it seems that most people who don't go to church think that Christianity is irrelevant and has nothing to offer them. And in the unlikely event they do dare to cross our church threshold, many church services often don't deliver what people are looking for. It doesn't scratch where they are itching.

What we think is urgently needed is something different, something that tries to think outside the box. This, unsurprisingly, is where Ignite comes in.

Ignite was born out of our passion to introduce Jesus to people in a way that made sense, in a way that wasn't hemmed in by 'churchy' words or traditions. We wanted to be real with people and somehow have honest and open conversations with them. This made us realise that what we were talking about was being intentionally relational with people. Getting to know people, making friends with them and loving them because God first loved us. The more we thought about it, the more stupidly obvious this need for relationship-building became.

Now, before you get all excited, we are not suggesting that Ignite is like some comic book caped crusader, swooping in and solving all these issues at once. If only that were true! However, we do think that Ignite is one way that we can at least begin to address the problems we are facing.

The Bible teaches us that God is relational. Jesus – God the Son – loves people! He went to where they were, he befriended them and he loved them intentionally. As a result, many were drawn to seek him out and listen while he talked about God. And he did it without being boring or irrelevant! So, if it was good enough for Jesus to do mission in this way, then maybe we should follow his example.

Which is what we have tried to do. I (Patrick) am an Anglican vicar, and I (Debbie) am a university counsellor and a missioner employed by Canterbury

Diocese. Our parish was one of the poorest in England, and our heart has always been for those who are marginalised and live within disadvantaged communities. However, our experience is that Ignite also works well within other socio-economic situations and with many different types of people: families, young people, children and so on.

We have divided this book into four sections. First, the DNA – what makes Ignite, Ignite? Second, the building blocks – the essential stuff you're going to need in place if you would like to set up an Ignite community. Third, the 'how to' bit – everything else you'll need (and need to know) to set up your very own weekly Ignite session. And then finally, the story of how Ignite began.

So, if your appetite for trying to do mission differently has been whetted by this little introduction, and you are up for a new adventure, then read on.

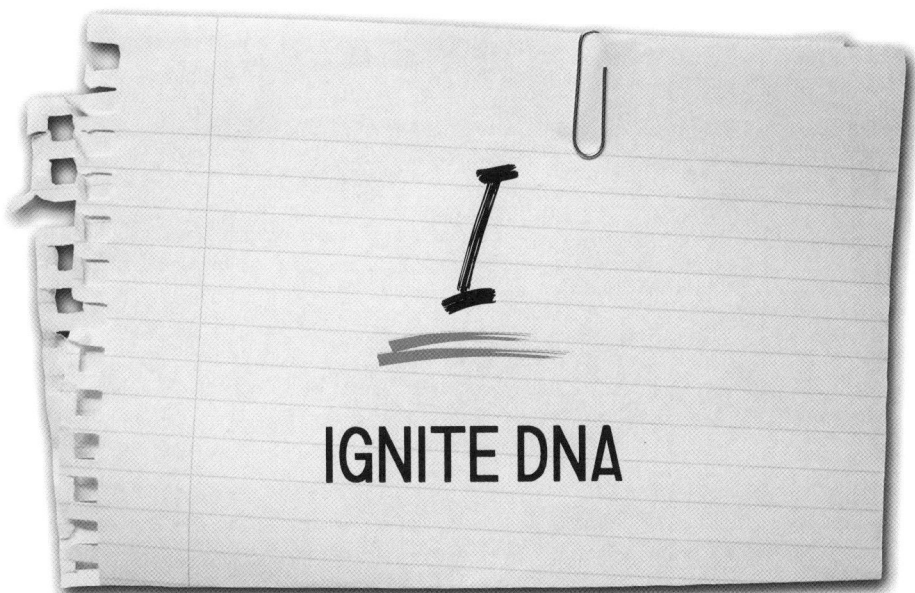

I

IGNITE DNA

1

It's church... but not as most people know it!

'And no one pours new wine into old wineskins. Otherwise, the wine will burst the skins, and both the wine and the wineskins will be ruined. No, they pour new wine into new wineskins.'

MARK 2:22 (NIV)

Those of us old enough to remember the original *Star Trek* series may recall Spock, when discovering a new lifeform, saying it's 'no life as we know it' – or, more likely, you may recall a close version of that line made popular by the song 'Star Trekkin''. Either way, we think it expresses a good way to think about what Ignite is like, or more accurately, what it isn't like!

Jesus said that the new wine of the kingdom needed new containers (wineskins); the old containers simply weren't up to the task. We wonder if some of our accepted ways of 'doing church' have become a little too inflexible over time, just like the old wineskins. Come with us as we experience a typical Ignite meeting.

Perhaps you arrived with a friend, wondering what you've let yourself in for. Or maybe you're on your own, but you've come because you overheard someone talking about this thing down at the local church called Ignite. The people there are supposed to be really nice, and you even get free cups of tea and food. So, you thought you'd be brave and give it a go, because you're a bit lonely and could do with some company.

Arriving at the church you immediately see a bright banner outside informing you that Ignite is on tonight. You read: 'Free food, lively chat and laughter!'

While you're waiting in the queue to go in, someone wearing a 'Team member' lanyard comes out and starts chatting with you. They share a joke and laugh, and then the queue starts moving forward and suddenly you're walking through the church doorway. Imagine that! You – in church! It's your first time since you were a child. Who'd have believed it? Inside, you're met by someone sat at a desk. They give you a big smiling 'Welcome', ask your name, which they then write on a sticky label, before handing it to you. 'Everyone wears one,' you're told, 'so we know each other's name. Go and grab yourself a cuppa and a hotdog.'

At first, you're not sure about the name label, but before long you've forgotten that you're even wearing it! After you've gotten your drink and food (and another welcome) from the person serving in the kitchen, another team member takes you to sit with them and a few other folks who are sat round a coffee table. That's a bit different, you think to yourself. They never had coffee tables in church when granny used to drag me to Sunday school.

You also notice that there's a few small cards lying on the table, with the words 'Please pray for…' The team member explains that if you've got anything going on in your life that you're worried about, such as health or money issues, or if you're worried about a friend or family member, you can write your concerns on one of the cards and someone from the church will pray for you at the next Sunday service. Introductions are made and pretty soon, you get drawn into the conversation.

After you've gotten yourself another cup of tea and eaten a couple more hotdogs, two team members get up on the stage, introduce themselves, welcome everyone to Ignite, and then say that there's going to be a music quiz and all the different coffee table groups are the different teams. You're quite pleased about that, as you love music! At the end of the quiz, your table group hasn't won, but you've enjoyed yourself.

Afterwards, two team members give some notices, including one about when a local food bank is open, which is really helpful, as your money's just run out for the week and you were wondering what you were going to do. Then, one of the team asks if anyone's got any encouragements to share. A few people put their hands up, and the other team member takes a microphone around. People share what good things have happened to them during the week, and everyone applauds whenever someone finishes talking.

After a while, you nervously put your own hand up, and when you're handed the mic, you say that you're new and how much you're enjoying being at Ignite. The team member who gave you the mic thanks you for your contribution and welcomes you to Ignite. You get a round of applause and suddenly you feel a little bit special and not quite so lonely.

Next, one of the team members on stage explains that you're going to play a game. They are going to read out catchphrases from different, famous people. And you and everyone else has to guess which famous person said that particular catchphrase. You manage to work out a few of them, including Bruce Forsyth's 'Nice to see you, to see you, nice!' because you used to really like Bruce.

Then you watch a funny video clip from an old TV series, *One Foot in the Grave*. That miserable bloke, Victor Meldrew, keeps saying, 'I don't believe it! I don't believe it!' when he gets himself into all sorts of silly situations.

After the video, one of the team members goes round and gives each of the table groups an envelope. Another team member explains that in the envelope there's a couple of verses from the Bible which have been cut up. Each table group has to see if they can put the words in the right order.

You haven't even looked at a Bible since you were a young lad, let alone read any of it. Still, no one seems that worried about it, and the team member who chatted to you outside, comes and sits with your group and helps to get the words sorted out. Apparently, it's about some bloke called Thomas, who didn't believe that Jesus had come back to life and wouldn't believe it unless he could put his finger in the holes where the nails went through Jesus. You get where Thomas was coming from, because you don't believe either. You suddenly realise that's a bit like Victor Meldrew's catchphrase.

Next, each table group are asked to chat among themselves about three questions. First, 'What sort of doubts stop people believing in God?' Then, 'Have you ever had doubts like Thomas?' And finally, 'What helps you believe?' You weren't too sure about the last two questions, but you chipped in about the first question, when you told the group that your mum had died quite young. You said that you couldn't believe in a God who took your mum before her time.

After talking about the questions, each group shares their answers. What surprises you is that even though, just like you, there are some people who don't believe in God, the team members leading the evening don't mind. It wasn't a problem that people didn't believe in God. They just thanked people for taking part in the discussion. It was like they were really interested in what you thought, even if you thought differently from them.

When the discussion was finished, a different team member got up on stage and summed up what the evening had all been about and what people had been talking about. And then they said something that caught your attention, even though you don't really know why. They said, 'Even if you don't believe in God, God still believes in you, because he loves you and thinks that you are very special!' Then they said that they were going to play a video song from some group called Sidewalk Prophets. You can't remember what it was called, but you do remember thinking, 'They never played music like that, when I went to church as a youngster! They were all boring hymns back then.'

After the song finished, one of the team members prayed a short prayer and then said that if anyone wanted a chat afterwards, to come and see them. But otherwise, they hoped that everyone would come back next week.

A couple of team members at the door chatted as you left and said how much they had enjoyed having you at Ignite. As you walked home, even though you weren't too sure about some of the God stuff, you thought you'd go back next week, because people had been nice to you, you'd had a laugh and you'd made some new friends. You never knew that church could be like that!

Reflection

How did I feel as I read about the Ignite meeting? Which bits would have made me feel anxious and which would have made me feel less worried, if I had been at the meeting as someone who doesn't go to church myself? Why might that be?

Prayer

Dear Lord, help me to remain open to you and to the work of the Holy Spirit. Where I have become set in my ways, keen to wander only down trusted pathways, may I be open to new things that you may have for me. May I be open to riding the rollercoaster with you! Amen.

2

Welcoming

Welcome one another, therefore, just as Christ has welcomed you, for the glory of God.
ROMANS 15:7 (NRSV)

There's a great song in the Disney film *Beauty and the Beast* called 'Be our guest'. Belle, the protagonist, is utterly and delightfully captivated by the intentional welcome that Lumière and the rest of the dinner service give her. So, now it's your turn to pull up a chair and be our guest, as we consider the importance of welcome at Ignite.

Genuinely welcoming people who come to an Ignite service is something we have worked hard to teach and encourage. We want everyone who has made the effort to walk through our doors to know that they are well and truly welcomed. We want them to feel the love. Why? Because being *welcomed well* really sticks in our memory. Whether it happens at a meeting, a friend's house, in a restaurant or wherever, a good welcome makes us feel appreciated, valued and at home.

Welcome is (almost) everything! It is crucial, because this interaction will determine whether the person comes back. This is why it needs to be sincere and honest. We are not welcoming people to get into their good books or get positive feedback on Tripadvisor. We do it because we think that's what Jesus would do. We do it because we actually like people and think that we have something worth sharing with them: friendship; an interest in who they are; the opportunity to discover Jesus at their pace, whenever they are ready to do so.

So we go out of our way to welcome people, to make them feel like they've come home. And we don't just do this at the door. Did you notice in the previous chapter how many times the person attending our imaginary Ignite service was welcomed in one way or another? In fact, without looking, have a guess as to how many times a welcoming-type engagement took place. The answer is at the end of this chapter.

We try, where possible, to start doing this before people have even come inside, and continue it throughout the time that people are with us, in different ways.

It starts with a team member chatting to guests waiting outside to come in, sharing a joke, passing the time of day, showing a friendly face and attitude that already breaks the ice. (Very bad jokes always seem to go down well, especially when it's raining.) It continues when they walk into church and are warmly greeted and handed a name badge, emphasising the fact that we want to get to know them. We don't want to remain strangers to each other.

The welcome carries on with cheerful volunteers in the kitchen serving free food and drinks. Then, throughout the rest of the service, 'welcome' plays a prominent role in all that we do. The two service leaders introduce themselves and welcome people. When the microphone is taken round for people to share encouragements, any new people who are brave enough to speak up are referred to by name and welcomed once again.

When Ignite ends, the service leaders intentionally thank people for having come and encourage them to come back next week. As people leave, other team members chat with them on the way out, mentioning that they are looking forward to seeing them again.

Which of these situations is more likely to encourage you to be a returning visitor:

a You are hardly noticed, the leaders and volunteers barely speak to you, and you are left to fend for yourself in terms of getting to know people.
b You are truly welcomed and valued, people are interested in you and pleased that you have turned up and they make you feel at home.

If we were betting people, our money would be on option 'b', because generally, people enjoy being appreciated. No one likes being an outsider or the odd one out, and so intentionally practising good welcoming goes a long way to help someone quickly feel like they belong.

Of course, if you can honestly say that your place of worship is already doing this, then that's amazing! We are so pleased that your church is committed to getting welcoming right. After all, Ignite does not have a monopoly on good practice.

But let's be honest. Many don't. Which means that in a time when church attendance continues to fall, for whatever reason, we must make the most of the opportunities that come our way. And by opportunities, we mean people! If someone dares to walk through our doors, then let's give them such a genuine, blatantly enthusiastic welcome, they will never forget it.

So, did you work out correctly that the number of welcoming interactions in chapter 1 was eight?

Reflection

Think of a few times when you have been made to feel really welcome somewhere or by someone. What contributed to that sense of welcome?

Do I create a sense of real welcome for others? What more could I do?

Prayer

Father God, we know that we are welcomed into your presence as friends. Help me to learn how to extend that welcome to all whom I encounter. Amen.

5

Belonging

As Jesus was walking beside the Sea of Galilee, he saw two brothers, Simon called Peter and his brother Andrew. They were casting a net into the lake, for they were fishermen. 'Come, follow me,' Jesus said, 'and I will send you out to fish for people.' At once they left their nets and followed him.

MATTHEW 4:18–20 (NIV)

In the 1968 film *Oliver!*, the Artful Dodger, when he first meets Oliver, bursts into a song about belonging and being part of the family. (We bet you'll be whistling the tune all day now!) Oliver is a young boy who's lost and who's looking for a new home, a new 'somewhere' to belong.

While we can't promise that our Ignite volunteers will burst into song every time a new guest walks through the doors, we do promise that everyone is treated like 'one of the family'.

Before we dive deeper into the concept of belonging in the context of Ignite, take a moment to think about how many groups or organisations you are a part of. Write them down now, as the number might surprise you.

Most people tend to belong to at least three, and likely more, different groups – family, church, work, friendship groups, hobby or fan clubs. The list could be very long!

Being part of a group, part of something bigger than just us as individuals, is good for us. We enjoy being with people who share similar views or experiences to our own. It gives us purpose, a reason for getting up in the morning.

This reminds us of another film that wonderfully demonstrates this. *The Full Monty* (1997) tells the story of six unemployed men, all quite different from each other, who meet at the local job club and team up to form a male striptease group to earn a bit of extra money. While the film is a comedy, what is both fascinating and at times deeply touching is the strong friendships that form between the men and the commitment that they have to each other.

When we belong to something, we make a connection to it. When we connect with others, we receive validation as a human being who is valued and accepted. This is such an important human need and is an area that many people who we have worked with at Ignite don't seem to have.

For some, family dynamics are difficult, causing them to be disconnected for a whole host of reasons – they've grown up in care or had family break-ups or long-standing arguments. Or perhaps they don't have a job, which restricts them in terms of who they meet. Finances might be tight, which means that they might not be able to join a club.

In fact, belonging is such an intrinsic human need and driving force, that some people who we meet at Ignite have previously formed relationships or joined 'groups' that are definitely not healthy and have caused them serious physical or mental harm. Perhaps they hang around with folk who commit petty crime. Or they develop a substance addiction.

For others, the need to belong to someone or something is so great that they allow themselves to be drawn into unhealthy, coercive relationships where they are taken advantage of. In these instances, Ignite can fill those gaps in their lives. It gives them a healthy, safe place to belong where they can express uncomfortable thoughts and grow in their understanding of themselves and how they relate to God.

All of which simply means that 'belonging' – being part of a group – is good for us. It can strengthen us both mentally and physically. It reminds us that we are valued and accepted. This is because we all seem to have a strong need and desire to belong. Most people don't like being outsiders or loners.

On the flip side human nature tends to be exclusive rather than inclusive. We easily divide into cliques and huddles that often become impenetrable to newcomers. Sadly, that is often the case in our churches as well.

At Ignite, however, we are not into cliques. We work hard at helping guests feel like they are home the moment they walk through our doors. Just as you read in chapter 1, we'll introduce a new person to some of our more established guests. We'll sit them down at a table group, maybe initially sitting with them until they feel at home.

In the Bible passage quoted at the beginning of chapter 3, Jesus calls his followers 'friends'. They were included. He made them insiders. Incredibly, he didn't wait until they (and we) became perfect or worthy of being friends. Jesus chose to create a sense of belonging and taught them to foster a right relationship with him and each other.

Jesus often created a sense of belonging. He did it with tax collectors, prostitutes and lepers. And at the very beginning of his ministry, he did it with a bunch of fishermen, when he said to them, 'Follow me.'

How might that inform, and perhaps transform, how we 'do church'?

We think that the standard model of church looks a bit like this:

Behave → Believe → Belong

There is an expectation that newcomers to church need to behave themselves or be 'good people'. Then they need to believe the things that we believe. Only after these two boxes have been ticked are they allowed to feel like they belong.

Like many more relational church thinkers, the Ignite model flips this round:

Belong → Believe → Behave

As people enjoy being part of Ignite (belonging) and experience more of God (believing), our hope is that, gradually, we will also see positive changes in their lifestyle or interaction with other people (behaviour). This reflects a changing from the inside outwards. But most importantly, whether or not behaviour changes, this isn't a condition of belonging. It doesn't mean that we will love them any less, not let them in or not want to befriend them. They find unconditional love and acceptance. There are no official or unofficial hoops to jump through or membership criteria to be met. People who come to Ignite automatically belong. (Behaviour that raises safeguarding concerns should always be dealt with appropriately, according to your own church's safeguarding policies.)

To underline the transformational power of belonging, we'd like to introduce you to one of our Ignite guests – let's call her Mandy (not her real name). A couple of years ago, the Church of England's Vision and Strategy team visited Ignite and made a short film presentation. In the film, they interviewed Mandy and several other Ignite guests. She spoke brilliantly about how much she valued the comfort of 'belonging' that Ignite gave her, and how later being baptised changed her life:

> I didn't go to church, I just went to the Ignite services. But it was fun, and I felt like I could be myself around people. My life just turned around when I got baptised. I never thought I would do anything like that, I was just so angry, messed up. But being baptised, the church turned my life around. They are always there for you, you know what I mean? You can always phone them or text them and they are there for you. I haven't got like a proper, real family, and to me this is my real family. If it wasn't for meeting them that day, you know, then I probably wouldn't be here today.

In terms of belonging, we don't think there's any better testimony! You can watch the whole video at **canterburydiocese.org/mission/ignite**.

Reflection

Where do I feel like I most belong? Why might that be?

Have I ever made anyone feel like an outsider? What could I have done differently?

Prayer

Jesus, I can see that you were an expert in helping people to feel that they belonged. If it was important for you, I want it to be important in what I'm doing. Amen.

6

Pursuing God

He has made everything beautiful in its time. He has also set eternity in the human heart; yet no one can fathom what God has done from beginning to end.
ECCLESIASTES 3:11 (NIV)

Patch Adams is a biographical comedy-drama film, set in the late 1960s/early 1970s and loosely based on the life of Dr Hunter 'Patch' Adams. At one point in the film, Patch says:

> *All of life is a coming home… Or as the poet Dante put it: 'In the middle of the journey of my life, I found myself in a dark wood, for I had lost the right path.' Eventually I would find the right path, but in the most unlikely place.*

The sentiment here is that life is about finding your way home; a journey, with twisty, sometimes wrong, turns and unexpected surprises, but worth pursuing, in order to get there. We think that home is discovering God's love for ourselves, and so at Ignite we unashamedly pursue him in all kinds of different ways.

We would love for anyone coming to Ignite to discover three things.

First, a respect and value for themselves.

Second, that they are valued and loved by others. This is why we concentrate so much on intentionally welcoming people, building meaningful relationships with them and creating an environment where they would be happy to belong. When you put all those together, Ignite already sounds like a great place to hang out.

However, amid of all that good stuff, the third thing that we absolutely want people who come to Ignite to discover is that God is real.

God really is real. Surprise! We want to demonstrate, in ways that make sense, that God is so much more than an exclamation word or a piece of jewellery. God is not a fairytale; God is not a work of fiction. Nor is God too good to be true. God is real, God loves people and God wants to be in a relationship with them. So at Ignite we help people to discover this by unashamedly pursuing God, sometimes subtly and other times not so subtly.

Mainstream churches have set out what they are about in fairly obvious ways. For example, if a non-believer plucks up the courage to go to a service, they are likely to sing various hymns or choruses, say some liturgical responses, be expected to listen (quietly) to a sermon for 15–45 minutes (or longer) and (also quietly) pray – or listen to – some prayers.

The problem with most of that is there is usually little room for the person who doesn't believe or the one who has questions. Belief feels like it's assumed, and questions are relegated to the back seat. And all that is often wrapped up in an environment where strangers are not welcomed well. Sadly, this leaves most non-Christians literally out in the cold.

At Ignite, we want people to feel at home. We want our environment to be a place where faith questions can be raised and answered in appropriate, relevant and fun ways. While our leaders and helpers are people of faith themselves, we don't presume that faith is in everyone else. We simply choose to talk about things in a way that allows us to gently share our faith and then see what happens.

In chapter 1, in our imaginary Ignite evening, we played a quiz about guessing famous people's catch phrases. This was then followed by a video clip from the old comedy TV show *One Foot in the Grave*, in which the lead character Victor Meldrew had the catch phrase 'I don't believe it!'

This is an example of Ignite doing what it does best. It was interactive, it created a bit of team bonding, it was fun and, most importantly, it enabled us to introduce 'Doubting' Thomas and his unwillingness to believe – in all his glory.

Here was a man, spoken about in the Bible, who *didn't* believe, just like many of our guests. More importantly, it showed that we – as faith practitioners – were not afraid to talk about doubts. It told our imaginary guests that it was okay to have doubts about faith and that we weren't expecting them to 'toe the party line'.

That was followed by something distinctly unsubtle – the asking of those three questions: 'What sort of doubts stop people believing about God?'; 'Have you ever had doubts like Thomas?'; 'What helps you believe?' These are big questions. However, the ground had already been prepared and softened by Ignite's safe, friendly environment, and by the earlier activities.

Suddenly, in small table groups, people were pursuing God! They might not have realised that was what they were doing, yet it was certainly the case. They were thinking about some deep theological questions in a way that made sense, in a way that wasn't threatening or made them feel like they weren't allowed to have a different opinion.

The evening was then topped off by a music video entitled 'I believe it now' by a Christian band called Sidewalk Prophets. If you hadn't already realised, this was an evening that we have done in real life, and where we played this song. The music video itself looks and sounds like one for any other decently made contemporary song. However, the lyrics are unashamedly Christian and thoughtfully honest. Using video gives people images that can help with focus; they are drawn to the screen. As we dim the surrounding lights the words enable people to continue pursuing God and better understand his love or deepen their relationship with him.

Using a well-chosen music video can often be helpful by giving people space to think about what has been shared during Ignite. In fact, for those who learn and understand more easily through visual or musical stimulation, it can help to connect them with God in ways that make more sense to them – although we also need to remember that it's important to vary our ways of offering opportunities for people to relate to God, because we are all different. God made us that way.

Then again, maybe the video *won't* help people connect. Just because we take people with us as we pursue God, doesn't mean that they are going to find or believe in God. Yes, someone might come to faith almost immediately, perhaps during the first time they come to Ignite – we've seen it happen – but, on the other hand, it might take months or years.

Or it might never happen. Who knows? What we *do* know is that pursuing God in the way we've described seems to make sense to people. Nothing is forced, honest conversation is encouraged, faith is explored and, all the while, the Holy Spirit is doing stuff and perhaps helping people, to quote Patch Adams again, to 'find the right path, but in the most unlikely place'.

Reflection

What is my preferred way of pursuing God? What helps me to push deeper into him? Is it through reading, listening to a sermon, watching a film or listening to a piece of music? Or something else?

Prayer

Dear God, I'm not just reading this book so I can help others begin to feel like they belong in your family; I also want to deepen my own sense of belonging. I want to know more deeply that I am your adopted child and that you love me beyond anything I can imagine. Amen.

Tea break

This seems like a good place to put the kettle on, have a cuppa and do a quick recap.

In chapter 1, we tried to give you an idea of what an Ignite evening feels like. Then, in the following five chapters, we outlined the various Ignite practices that bring an Ignite evening to life. Ignite is *welcoming, relational, interactive*, a place where you feel that you *belong* and works hard to *actively pursue God.*

And to top it all – amazingly – you've not been put off yet!

In fact, you might be thinking that you can see real value in what we've been sharing. Maybe you've also had one of those Holy Spirit 'itches', where it feels like God is prompting you to get involved, to do something. Maybe, you are also thinking that you'd like to start an Ignite service yourself. If that's the case, fantastic! The next chapter is definitely for you.

However, if that's not the case, and you're not really feeling it yet, then that's also okay. We won't cross you off our Christmas card list or think any less of you. We understand that not everyone is called to get involved with Ignite.

But we'd still like to encourage you to keep reading, because as you do, God may bring to mind someone who would be great at doing this Ignite stuff and who you think really needs to read this book.

Either way, finish your cuppa, munch on a biscuit and take a few moments to reflect on what you've read so far and what God might be wanting to reveal to you.

II

IGNITE BUILDING BLOCKS

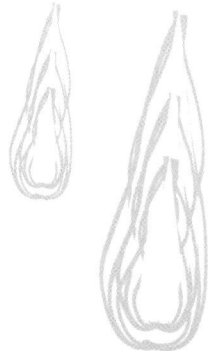

7

Building the team

'For where two or three gather in my name, there am I with them.'
MATTHEW 18:20 (NIV)

In the film *Facing the Giants*, Grant Taylor, the coach of a struggling high school American football team, presents his team with a new approach to playing football, telling them:

> *'If we win, we praise him. And if we lose, we praise him. Either way, we honour him with our actions and our attitudes. So, I'm asking you: what are you living for? I've resolved to give God everything I've got. Then I'll leave the results up to him. I want to know if you'll join me?'*

We think it's a great philosophy for an Ignite team; we want God to bless our Ignite team so much that people in the community will talk about it. If we succeed, we praise him. And if we don't, we praise him. Either way, we honour him with our actions and our attitudes.

The game Jenga derives its name from the Swahili word *kujenga*, which means 'to build'. Traditionally Jenga is played with 54 wooden blocks stacked into a tower, as you move the brick out of the pile and place them on to the top, you're aiming to increase the height of the tower without the pile collapsing!

We have often played Jenga at Ignite social events and it's fascinating to see how carefully individuals move blocks around. They think about it, they assess the 'wobble factor', they pause and consider every move looking at the structure from different angles before they make any changes. We see gestures of praying hands and looks to heaven for divine inspiration before making their decisions – they really don't want the blocks to fall! We could go a long way with this analogy, but you probably get the point.

When it comes to building and supporting a team, we think it's best to have an approach that is like playing Jenga. We too need to pray and look for divine inspiration, because we want to create a team that is going to be cohesive and well built. We want a team which won't fall down easily. We want a team that 'lives out its faith', as the coach in *Facing the Giants* states so clearly.

There is, however, an important point to state here, albeit an obvious one – the team is made up of people with their own thoughts and feelings. They are not just 'Jenga blocks' in our game. People are shaped differently; they have differing strengths and weaknesses; they have different interests and so they bring different skills to our team.

In our view a good team shouldn't all look the same! Ignite needs people who are passionate about prayer walking, people who enjoy cooking meals and washing-up, people who are fit and able to move chairs and tables around, and people who know how to use audiovisual equipment. And don't forget those who are willing to stand up front and deliver the planned material, those who will go shopping for food and equipment, and those who are comfortable talking to people they don't know.

Don't forget that roles can overlap – a person can welcome people and wash up. So don't panic – you don't need a team of 15 people! The most important thing is that everyone needs to work together to form a supportive and effective Ignite team structure. Team members can be drawn just from your own church, but it's much better if a team is made up of members from several different churches within the local area who you have connections with.

The Bible reminds us that God loves it when we work together:

> For we are fellow workers in God's service; you are God's field, God's building.
> 1 CORINTHIANS 3:9 (NIV)

How good and how pleasant it is when God's people live together in unity!
PSALM 133:1 (NIV)

On a practical note, we give team members lanyards for their name labels. These show individuals as belonging to a team but most importantly it means guests can easily find a team member if they need one. This gives us strength and helps to create a safer environment for everyone.

We also love the fact that Ignite team members can be at different stages in their faith journeys. For example, a fairly new Christian may have a life that seems less 'sorted' than more mature Christians, but they may have a newly fired-up passion for the gospel that is infectious and draws others in. It may also be that others find it easier to see themselves in newer Christians and find that aspect of them more relatable – that we do not need to be fully sorted to work for God, just willing to allow him to work in us and through us. Building a diverse team creates strength and allows others to see people like them in those leadership roles.

However, the team should *always* be made up of at least three or four Christians who are well established in their faith. They need to be Ignite's spiritual guardians – the ones who will be help keep the team on a spiritual even keel. This in turn creates the solid faith foundation on which an Ignite community can be built and can flourish.

During the process of replicating Ignite within Canterbury Diocese and into Guernsey, we have seen a clear link between Ignite having active clergy involvement and its success. Where clergy have not been involved, the communities have struggled. This doesn't mean that ordained church leaders are necessarily the most gifted in working within Ignite, although some are; rather, church backing is a powerful contingent in a successful outcome. So we suggest that you have a strong connection with the parochial church council (PCC) or other leadership structure.

Apart from the importance of creating a team made up of 'varied shapes', it's also important that both you and your team members are up for the challenge of building genuine, no-strings attached relationships. We are blessed that Ignite often attracts some of the more 'demanding' people from our communities, maybe because they are more aware of their need to connect. Relationship-building is a real honour, and to be able to support people when they feel at their most vulnerable and connect with God is amazing. But it is also time-consuming and hard work. So, as much as you can, be very sure that this is what you believe God is calling you and your team to do. Don't be tempted to launch into Ignite until you've done the legwork within the community, which we will talk about later in the book.

Continuity is important. Nobody wants people being befriended at Ignite, where they start to develop a sense of self-worth, only to discover a few weeks later that the team member who befriended them has suddenly left. How is that going to potentially leave them feeling? Betrayed? A bit cross, perhaps? Or maybe left thinking that it's their fault? That's not what we would want for anybody. So be prepared to be in it for the long haul, if possible.

Reflection

Who do I know who God might be calling to be part of an Ignite team? Who has got a similar love for the local community?

Who could be the spiritual guardians?

Prayer

Father God, if you are calling me to start Ignite in my community, please show me who you are also calling, that we might build an effective team together. Amen.

8

Prayer

Pray hard and long. Pray for your brothers and sisters. Keep your eyes open.

EPHESIANS 6:18 (MSG)

> *'We do not pray to tell God what he does not know, nor to remind him of things he has forgotten. He already cares for the things we pray about… He has simply been waiting for us to care about them with him.'*
>
> Philip Yancey, *Prayer: Does it make any difference?* (Hodder & Stoughton, 2006)

Sadly, we couldn't find any films that floated our boat about the importance of prayer from an Ignite perspective. However, we think that Philip Yancey's quote is both helpful and accurate. It's time to move out into our local community and start praying and caring about the stuff that God cares about.

If the first section of this book is all about the Ignite building blocks, then prayer is surely the foundation stone. It's the essential, overarching ingredient that needs to be present in all that we do as we start engaging with the community where we would like to launch an Ignite service.

Before we write anything else, however, we will say that *we know* that *you know* that prayer is vital. We also know that many amazing people, far more capable than us, have written fantastic books about the importance of prayer: why, when, where and how to do it. We know that you are likely to have read much of that good stuff.

We also understand that you are probably as massively passionate about your relationship with God as you are about your love for your community. But we can't stress enough how crucial prayer is, especially at this early stage in building and launching an Ignite service. Which means that, while there's not much need for us to go on about prayer too much, we do want to mention a few things.

Psalm 127 reminds us that, 'Unless the Lord builds the house, the builders labour in vain' (v. 1, NIV). We do nothing on our own. Indeed, if we do, we might as well pack up and go home, because we are not going to get anywhere.

We are partners with God, and through prayer we listen and talk to God. We share with God our hopes and our longings for our community. We allow ourselves to be guided to the places and people that God wants us to engage with.

What this looks like in real life is obviously going to vary from person to person, so we can only speak from our own experience. In our church, for example, there was a mid-week prayer meeting. When we knew we were going to try to replicate Ignite, we sort of hijacked the group (in a good way), in that a large part of the group's time was spent praying for anything to do with Ignite and with those who were doing the replication. Perhaps you have a similar group in your own church?

If we all accept that prayer is so important, please don't let it become just an afterthought. Don't stick it on at the end of a meeting because that's what you're supposed to do. Instead, pray like it's going out of fashion! Pray for Ignite individually, pray within a small group and pray as a church. Give the church regular updates about what's happening with the Ignite initiatives – be excited about what God is doing in your community and share your excitement with others. *Be* excitement in your church – it's infectious! Get Ignite put on your church leadership's agenda as a standing item, so it's prayed for every time they meet.

One of the most important things you can do is to pray while you're walking around the community where you believe God is calling you to establish an Ignite service. Our good friend the Revd Steve Coneys has often described this as being 'detectives of divinity'. We need to have our eyes and ears open to discern (detect) what God is doing in our local community or who he wants us to have an encounter with. And when we spot what God's doing, then if appropriate, we need to be brave and join in with it.

There's a great illustration of being a 'divinity detective' in the story of Philip and the Ethiopian eunuch (Acts 8:26–40). We've already agreed that part of partnering with God in prayer is listening to him, and that is exactly what Philip was doing. He's got his 'detective of divinity' hat on, and so he hears the Holy Spirit telling him to, 'Go to that chariot and stay near it' (v. 29). Philip obeys, and the rest is history.

By asking a simple question – 'Do you understand what you are reading?' (v. 30) – Philip is given the opportunity to share 'the good news about Jesus' (v. 35). This leads to the eunuch being baptised, who then goes on his way rejoicing. It's a fabulous story about how such divine encounters can change a person's life.

While we don't think that you are likely to an encounter a chariot-riding Ethiopian eunuch yourself, we think that as you go about prayerfully within your local community, there will be plenty of opportunities to join in with the stuff that God is leading you to.

For example, maybe while you are prayer walking you encounter someone sat alone on a bench. You casually say hello, and then in true British style comment on the weather. At this point you will probably know if the person is happy to talk to you. Remember, you have asked God to take you where he wants you to go, so trust the process. If it feels right, continue to chat, follow their lead on what they want to talk about. It needs to be their agenda, not yours. Keep the conversation natural and be interested in them and what they are saying. This may just end up being a one-off conversation with someone from the community who you never meet again. You simply had a pleasant conversation with somebody, which is great. However, within the conversation, the person may share something personal or important to them, which may cause you to say that you are a Christian and offer to pray for them. If they say, 'No, thanks', be accepting of that and just see where the rest of the conversation goes. But, if they say, 'Yes', then keep the prayer very short, simple and without 'churchy' words. They just need to know that God loves them and cares for their needs.

At the end of the day, all that you have to do is pray that God leads you to the right people and into the right situations and that God would grant you favour as you do this. Pray that God's Spirit would be at work in the most unexpected of places. Pray for local community transformation.

Above all, keep going even after Ignite is launched in your community. Don't stop and don't give up!

Reflection

What needs within my local community am I already aware of, that I could be praying about?

How could I pray both differently and creatively for my community?

Prayer

Lord Jesus, help me to be excited about the power of prayer and enable me to communicate that excitement to members of my church. Please fan into flame my desire to pray more passionately and frequently for my local community, so as I go about my daily life, I may become a better detective of divinity! Amen.

9

Building links with your community (no strings attached)

'Let me tell you why you are here. You're here to be salt-seasoning that brings out the God-flavours of this earth… Here's another way to put it: You're here to be light, bringing out the God-colours in the world. God is not a secret to be kept. We're going public with this, as public as a city on a hill. If I make you light-bearers, you don't think I'm going to hide you under a bucket, do you? I'm putting you on a light stand. Now that I've put you there on a hilltop, on a light stand – shine! Keep open house; be generous with your lives. By opening up to others, you'll prompt people to open up with God, this generous Father in heaven.'

MATTHEW 5:13–16 (MSG)

In the film *Run Fatboy Run*, Dennis (played by Simon Pegg) wants to win back the woman that he originally jilted at the altar, and so decides to try to impress her by running the London marathon. Early on in the film, as he begins his training and preparation, he asks his friend Gordon if there is some special technique to running. 'Well, yeah,' Gordon replies. 'You put one leg in front of the other, over and over again, really, really fast.'

Sometimes, the best advice is really obvious.

You may be reading this book knowing that you go to a church, or even lead a church, where a considerable part of your community doesn't go to church – although that's hardly surprising, as most people don't go to church.

You may have also sat in many meetings which looked at how you could encourage those very same people to walk through the church doors and have an opportunity to discover God for themselves. Again, most churches who have a passion for their community have done this in one way or another. We advertise and hold all manner of events, and we ask church members to invite family, friends and neighbours to entice people in.

However, jumble sales, coffee mornings, church fetes and even the various courses that are on offer exploring Christianity don't seem to be having a great deal of success in the enticing department. It may have something to do with the fact that scripture is a bit quiet on enticing people into church, to worship. You were more likely to find Jesus out and about, telling people about God and his amazing kingdom. He moved around a lot, meeting up with all manner of different people: tax collectors, lepers, fishermen, Pharisees, to name but a few. These were real people with real issues or problems or questions, and Jesus met with them – where they were – and did real life with them.

Take a few moments to read through the first couple of chapters of Mark's gospel and count how many different people Jesus interacts with. Don't just count the folk who are named or had a starring role, like the paralysed man; also include the little groups and the big crowds – do some guess work about their size. Jesus wasn't just out and about – he was busily out and about!

And let's not forget Jesus' final words to his disciples: 'Therefore go and make disciples of all nations' (Matthew 28:19, NIV). The Ignite model values this verse because it helps us to understand that we must first go out into our local community. However, we don't go out purely to bring them in. We go out to where the people are, to get involved, to be seen, to enable people to get to know us – and us them.

Some of the questions we need to be asking are: who are the community's 'movers and shakers'? Who are the local trusted people or 'people of peace'? It's important to answer these questions because we try to support and encourage what they do. Why? Because we are not setting ourselves up in competition with them. Rather, our hope and prayers are that gradually we can work together for the betterment of that community. They have good things to offer people, and so do we! So we trust God to go ahead of us, preparing hearts for these new connections.

When we think back to the relational and interactive nature of Ignite, it would be strange to expect a person to come to an event by means of a poster. Yes, a few might come, but most people won't. The reality is that we need to go and – like Dennis from our film quote – 'put one leg in front of the other, over and over again'. We need to get out into the real world, where the people are. In the process of going out we make new relationships and can often create a sense of belonging before a person even walks through the church door.

As we later discuss in chapter 16, 'How it all began', Ignite started in Cliftonville, Margate, almost accidentally, through a process of long-term engagement with the local community. However, when we first replicated Ignite it was a much more intentional process. The second Ignite was started by Debbie and Captain Stuart Budden, our Church Army colleague. We will use some of our experiences from this replication to show how we intentionally built links with this community.

In the first six-to-nine months before starting any Ignite events, the emphasis needs to be on building relationships, both within the local church families and with the local community. In both cases, the main aim is to establish trust and friendship. We need to take our 'light out from under the bucket.' Right from the outset, the Ignite model is relational in its approach.

We need to be visible in our communities as individuals so that we become both known and trusted. It's important that church members are active, visible and known within their community, maybe by joining committees, attending sports events, supporting local events or helping to run the local food bank or charity shop, for example. So often we get so busy with doing things within our churches that we become less present within other community events. We need to be salt and light in the world, not just within our church walls.

And so, we do our research, and we get involved. When do other community events happen? What's bothering people? What do they struggle with? What's happening in the community today? What are its aspirations for the future? What sort of history does the community have? By doing this, we begin to understand what people are thinking and feeling.

Here's some examples of what we found out when we started researching the local area in preparation for replicating Ignite for the first time.

We met a lady who ran the local post office, and she was amazing. She knew everyone and everything that went on. People shared their concerns with her and trusted her; more importantly for us she came to know and trust us. This in turn gave us a 'passport' of authority within the community. By her telling local people that we were 'good people', we gained a local acceptance that would otherwise have taken us ages to earn on our own.

We found out that 40 or so years earlier, the local area was renowned for high levels of crime and violence. Forty years later, even though crime and violence were no longer anywhere near what they used to be, the area still had a bad name. Consequently, it affected how the people who lived there thought of themselves.

We also discovered that the community was heavily involved in building the parish church. At that time, many people 'bought a brick'. This gave them a long-standing and deep sense of church ownership. When we were out and about in the community, we would often hear people talk about 'our church' even though they may not have set foot in the building for years, if ever. People already felt like they belonged, and it was something we knew we could build on.

Finally, just by listening we were able to learn their needs. People told us they were really unhappy about all the litter that was lying around the streets. They were also frustrated that they couldn't afford to pay the fee that the local council charged for removing unwanted furniture from their homes. And because many of the residents didn't own cars, they couldn't move it themselves, which meant that this furniture was left sitting in people's front gardens for weeks, sometimes even months, at a time. People were overwhelmed by the situation and felt defeated. So we decided to be proactive and do something about it.

We started walking round the area, doing litter picks and praying as we worked. We also took some of the unwanted furniture to the local tip. Many people were genuinely baffled as to why we would do such a thing, but it generated some great conversations and earned us bucket loads of local respect.

All our knowledge of this community's needs, its history and its DNA fell into our laps just by talking to people. None of it was particularly evangelistic; we weren't Bible thumping or shouting about Jesus from street corners. We were just being salt and light and bringing the life-enhancing distinctiveness and flavour of Christ into the mix. This gradually changed the narrative from 'them and us' into just 'us'. We never hid that we were Christians, but we never made a big deal of it either. Their community became our community, and suddenly we were living life together.

The really interesting thing is that, while doing all this, finding out about what made the community tick, and getting ourselves known and trusted, people eventually started seeking us out. They'd track us down just to have a chat with us because they liked us. Or they'd share a problem with us. Or they'd come and find us to ask for help with something. Some even came wanting to understand faith more, to talk about their grapples with life's purpose. And as they asked, we shared.

We moved from being 'those people from the church' to 'Stuart and Debbie', and we built real relationships, no strings attached. This is what we call a pivotal point. It's the point in which people within the community start looking to us for friendship and to support them with their needs. At this stage, even though they don't realise it, they are experiencing God's grace and generosity, and they are connecting with faith.

When this happens, we think it's the right time to start holding Ignite events.

Reflection

How well do you know your local community? What do they need? Let's find out!

Who are the 'people of peace' or the 'movers and shakers'? Who are the local community leaders? Have you got a local community policeman or PCSO? Who are they?

Where is the local community centre? Who manages it and what goes on there? What about local businesses – are there local shops you could support? What challenges are they facing?

Prayer

Father God, give me eyes to see and ears to hear what you are doing in my community, and help me to join in with what you are doing. Amen.

10
Social events

So, I recommend having fun, because there is nothing better for people in this world than to eat, drink, and enjoy life. That way they will experience some happiness along with all the hard work God gives them under the sun.

ECCLESIASTES 8:15 (NLT)

One of our favourite bits in the animated film *Madagascar* is when Marty, Melman and Gloria stumble across a huge group of lemurs having a party. It's a complete riot of fun, dance and living life to the full. And then King Julien appears on the scene and memorably breaks into a rendition of 'I Like To Move It'. And everyone enthusiastically shouts back: 'Move it!'

Those lemurs definitely know how to enjoy themselves. And while Ignite social events may not be in quite the same league as a lemur dance night, they are certainly the best of times when it comes to having fun, and more importantly, deepening and strengthening community relationships. So let the party begin, and 'Move it!'

People have always found it challenging to transition from what they know into something new or unfamiliar, such as moving to a new job or new school. People generally like what they are familiar with and take a while to get used to new environments. As an Ignite team we need to understand this.

Somehow, we need to create a bridge that helps people transition from them meeting us out on the streets as we engage with them within the community to them feeling safe and comfortable in a church.

The first very important part of that bridge (or transition) is you and others in your team and the relationship that you have built with the people. The second thing that helps to smooth this transition process is 'social events and food'.

People generally feel more comfortable coming into an unfamiliar environment if (a) they know someone who is going to be there, who will welcome them and sit with them, and (b) if there is a user-friendly, familiar social event happening that they feel comfortable with.

Let's set the scene for a moment. You're at the point where you and/or your volunteers have built a good rapport with some of the local residents. In fact, because people know when you're likely to be at certain places within the community, some of them have started to seek you out. Now is the time to begin planning for your first Ignite social event and start handing out invites.

At this point, it's important to be strategic about how you invite people. Use the local 'movers and shakers' that you have identified and let them do much of the inviting. Invite the people that you have got to know and tell them it would be great for them to bring their family or friends as well if they want to. Get posters up in local shops, and deliver leaflets to people's houses, if you think that would be helpful (but don't think that doing so will attract loads of people; it won't). Above all, talk to people about the event and do so with loads of energy and enthusiasm. If it doesn't sound interesting, they are less likely to come.

It is important that all events are welcoming, free and generous. If you need to, seek funding from elsewhere but not from those we are drawing into church. We need to be building bridges to friendship and faith, rather than confirming suspicions that the church is only interested in their money.

For our social events, we have held BBQs, quiz nights and bingo evenings, to name but a few. No doubt, you can think of some others. We've even put on a live band playing only secular music.

Right from the start, be sure to use the Ignite name: 'Ignite BBQ', 'Ignite Quiz', 'Ignite Bingo' and so on. You are trying to embed the name Ignite into people's consciousness, and if you use the name, then others will as well and it will become familiar to them.

If you choose to do an 'Ignite Quiz', make sure it is accessible to everyone. This is not the time to discover who has the greatest knowledge of sport or music. It is important that people don't leave feeling stupid! Film observation quizzes or multiple-choice quizzes can be helpful in preventing this. Instead, it's the time to be encouraging conversation between people and small table groups. The aim is for people to leave feeling built up in their confidence, relaxed and connected with others. If they leave with these feelings, they are much more likely to return.

Within the social event it works well to have an activity that collects people's contact details. Simple activities like 'guess the number of sweets in the jar' or 'guess the weight of the cake'. Always be clear about how the data will be stored and used, and make sure you're complying with General Data Protection Regulation; a simple tick box asking 'Would you like to be informed about future Ignite events?' is a useful way of building up future contacts.

All social events should run in a similar way to an Ignite evening: name labels should be used, grace said before food and it should never be hidden that we are a community of faith. Although we start with social events, it is important that you don't do too many. Just do two or three events a few weeks apart before you start to use the Ignite teaching series. If you do too many, people will start to see Ignite as a community that only holds social events and they will resent changing when you start using the teaching material.

Social events will remain an important part of Ignite. We tend to have them in between the end of one teaching series and the beginning of another. We also use them to draw people back into Ignite, after Christmas or Easter breaks.

Remember: keep social events fun, friendly, generous and free!

Reflection

What sort of community events are successful in my local area? Quiz nights? Karaoke nights? BBQs?

How do I feel about potentially running a bingo evening? (In other words, does my church have a problem with bingo, because it is viewed as gambling?)

Prayer

Lord Jesus, as we meet and socialise with others help us to see how you delight in them. We pray that those who come will be relaxed in the church and feel like they belong. Amen.

11

Planning an Ignite service

Careful planning puts you ahead in the long run; hurry and scurry puts you further behind.

PROVERBS 21:5 (MSG)

We love the film *Elf*. We particularly like how Buddy (the eponymous elf) is so enthusiastic about everything he sees and does. A perfect example of this is how he goes about planning a day out with his dad, starting with making snow angels for two hours, followed by ice skating, then eating through a roll of cookie dough as fast as they can. 'And then,' he says, 'to finish, we'll snuggle.'

Buddy is determined to have a great day with his dad, so his planning has been meticulous. Needless to say, Dad isn't impressed, and is being a bit of a grouch, which is probably why he's on the 'naughty list'!

However, as far as we're concerned, Buddy's planning is awesome, although we think we'd have the cookie dough hot with ice cream. Apart from that, Buddy has clearly given his plans a great deal of thought. Which leads us nicely into our next chapter.

An Ignite team should be looked after in much the same way as those who come along to an Ignite event. That is, through welcoming hospitality, we value our team members and walk with them on their faith journey. For us this means doing community with them. It means sharing our lives with them. It also means that we mirror the hospitality that is shown at Ignite.

For planning meetings, therefore, we invite the whole team to our house. For some of us, this might not sound that important. But it is! Inviting the team to our home says that we value them and are happy to share our home with them. It elevates the meeting from being just a business meeting to something more personal, more relaxed and ultimately – we hope – more productive in terms of what we achieve together.

We hold our planning meetings weekly, as it helps to keep our content alive in a way that monthly or termly planning never can. It's better to invite everyone on the team to the planning meeting; otherwise you risk creating a two-tiered team – those who lead and those who 'just help'. It's more inclusive for team members to decide themselves about their level of involvement. This leads more easily to capable but nervous people developing and taking up a more 'up front' role.

We found that, although all are invited, only some of the team come every week, others occasionally and others not at all. An all-are-welcome approach builds team community and allows everyone to be more aware of the content of the evenings and offer valuable and varied input into the programme.

Before we do any planning, we get into the important job of eating together! Sometimes that is a full meal; other times it is just soup or cakes. The point is that we are spending time together, chatting, laughing and generally enjoying each other's company. This builds deeper friendship and trust and helps us to get to know each other a little bit better.

Planning usually follows a similar weekly structure that allows us to both learn from what we have done and to also plan in response to the needs of our Ignite community. After opening in prayer, we always start by looking back at the previous week's Ignite meeting, asking ourselves: what went well and what not so well? What problems were there? What about any victories or breakthroughs? How well were our guests engaging? Does anybody need more personal support? This keeps our thinking and planning up to date and relevant.

Next, we revisit what we have already planned at the previous planning meeting for this week's coming Ignite evening. Are we still happy with it? Do we need to make any changes in the light of how Ignite went last week? We then share out the jobs for the coming week so that we know who is responsible for what, and we think about anything we need to buy.

Finally, we start to plan the following weeks' running order, laying down the structure for the evening before we close in prayer.

Throughout this process, we make sure that within any of our planning, there is a variety of things that will hold people's attention in different ways during Ignite. We are constantly doing a balancing act – have we used enough film clips or have we used too many? Should we have a drama sketch this week? What's the Christian content like – too heavy or too light? Is there enough space for the serious stuff as well as the fun stuff? Are there opportunities for guests to respond in prayer, if appropriate?

Finally, with this chapter just about done, it's time for us to confess. When we were going out into our community our prayer focus was very strong; it was almost like we were preparing to do battle with the gods of this world. We prayed before we went out, we prayed while we were walking around – you get the picture. However, when we were in our own safe territory, planning an Ignite evening, probably because we often worried about taking up too much of the team's time, prayer often became short and functional. Consequently, prayer slipped down the priority list.

So, here's an honest plea: learn from us and do better. Please, prioritise prayer in your planning meetings!

While Ephesians 3:20 reminds us that God can do so much more than we ask or imagine, we are also instructed to 'commit everything you do to the Lord. Trust him, and he will help you' (Psalm 37:5, NLT). Make sure you prioritise committing everything to God. Ensuring that Christ is the foundation, a strong, stable, outward-facing leadership team supplies stable building blocks for others to place themselves on to. In turn, this makes it more likely that they will pattern their lives on what they see.

Reflection

How do I feel about using my home for showing hospitality to my team, as well as for regular planning meetings?

What strengths do I bring to the planning process? Creativity, eye for detail, hospitality facilitator or something else? What might my weaknesses be? Easily distracted by the need to 'look after' people in my home? Difficulty in getting the right balance mixing business and hospitality?

Prayer

Dear Father, please help me plan effectively, allowing myself to be directed towards whatever you want me to accomplish for Ignite. Help my planning ideas be in line with yours, so that in all things, your will be done. In Jesus' name. Amen.

Tea break

Any biscuits left from the last tea break?

We hope so, because having successfully completed your quest in getting to the end of part II, we thought you might be ready for another break, while we do another recap. Chocolate digestive, anyone?

We briefly touched on the importance of prayer. We didn't want to labour the point, because hopefully we're all Christians who understand that prayer is a big deal. However, neither did we want to ignore it and thereby possibly give the wrong message. So, to reiterate the last line of that chapter: don't stop and don't give up!

We then looked at some of the ways of building no-strings-attached links with your local community. Within this group of chapters, we bet this is the one that either excited you or terrified you the most. If you were excited, then great! It sounds like this is just the book for you, and maybe we should sit down and have a conversation together soon.

However, if you were terrified, then, bizarrely, that's also great! This book is meant to challenge as much as it's meant to inspire. Sometimes us timid ones – that's how Patrick would describe himself; Debbie's the chatterbox (sit her next to someone on a park bench, and within five minutes she'll know their entire life story) – need to be reminded of these words from Isaiah:

> For I, the Lord your God, hold your right hand; it is I who say to you, 'Do not fear, I will help you.'
> ISAIAH 41:13 (NRSV)

Doing Ignite, engaging with the community, prayer walking the streets, and so on is not just for the Tiggers of this world (the bouncy, outgoing and self-confident tiger from *Winnie the Pooh*); it's for whoever God calls to do this stuff, even those of us who are part of the timid Piglet brigade.

In the section on team building, we were reminded that 'people are shaped differently; they have differing strengths and weaknesses; they have different interests and so they bring different skills to our team' (p. 38).

Finally, we arrived at the nitty-gritty of how to plan an actual Ignite session.

Our tea break is nearly over, and pretty much all the chocolate digestives are gone. So, as you finish off your tea, have a look back at those parts of the last section that resonated with you and also those you struggled with. What is God trying to teach you, and who could you talk to about it?

III

PRACTICALITIES

12

Food

The Lord appeared to Abraham near the great trees of Mamre while he was sitting at the entrance to his tent in the heat of the day. Abraham looked up and saw three men standing nearby. When he saw them, he hurried from the entrance of his tent to meet them and bowed low to the ground. He said, 'If I have found favour in your eyes, my lord, do not pass your servant by. Let a little water be brought, and then you may all wash your feet and rest under this tree. Let me get you something to eat, so you can be refreshed and then go on your way – now that you have come to your servant.'

GENESIS 18:1–5 (NIV)

In series 3, episode 8 of *The Chosen*, we see that Jesus (wonderfully played by Jonathan Roumie) has been speaking to an enormous crowd, literally thousands of people.

He says to them, 'I kept you here all this time giving you spiritual food. But you clearly need actual food now. So, let's eat!' As he says, 'Let's eat', with a big smile on his face, a huge cheer erupts from the crowd, followed by clapping and laughter as the disciples distribute the miraculously multiplied bread and fish. The scene is a brilliantly portrayed picture of good times and people enjoying each other's company around food.

How we wish we could have been there ourselves. But we do have the next best thing: socialising and eating with some friends – at Ignite, obviously.

Food always seemed to play a big part in Jesus' ministry. In the gospels Jesus is often described as eating with all sorts of people: sinners and tax collectors; Pharisees; his friends; even people he didn't know. We are happy to follow his lead.

Unsurprisingly, this means that food is also important at Ignite. We welcome people with loads of warm drinks and food on offer. We may keep it cheap and cheerful, but we also keep it plentiful. Many of our Ignite communities have been run in parishes where there are multiple levels of deprivation. For these people, being provided with hot food and drinks can mean that we are meeting one of their basic human needs, as well as following Jesus' teaching: 'I was hungry and you gave me something to eat, I was thirsty and you gave me something to drink, I was a stranger and you invited me in' (Matthew 25:35, NIV). So, it's a no-brainer – by feeding those in need we are feeding and welcoming Jesus.

For others who come to Ignite, food might not be an immediate or desperate need. Maybe they have enough. However, even if we are just able to sit down round a table having a hot drink together, we are being community. When you generously share food and drink with others, you are making a public declaration about Christianity's spirit of generosity and welcome. You are demonstrating sacrificial love, something that is absolutely worth investing in.

Some weeks we just supply simple food, such as cakes or doughnuts that can be eaten quite quickly. Other weeks we serve up a full hot meal. You will see this reflected in the Ignite running orders later, where we allow either 30 minutes or an hour at the start of an evening for food.

We always start with food and drinks to welcome people in. We know that many other outreach projects do this the other way round – in other words, people come to the event, they get the teaching bit and then food is shared.

However, that doesn't sit well with us. We don't want people to feel that they must sit through something just to get a meal – that could create feelings of resentment, which is not the best way to start a relationship. Also, if you're hungry or thirsty, your attention is going to be affected. You're going to struggle to concentrate and enjoy an Ignite evening if your stomach is rumbling.

A common objection that is raised to providing food at the start is that people will simply come to Ignite for the food and drink and then leave. This is something that has been often said to us. Yes, some people may use us as a place to get free food. If so, then great! If people come and eat with us, feel welcomed and are allowed to leave when they are ready, without any judgement, then they generally come back, which gives us more opportunities to build relationships with them.

In our experience, some people definitely do just stay for the food, so they come again. Next time they do, volunteers act like they've known them for years and welcome them back. They start getting comfortable with being at Ignite in church. Eventually, they start staying longer, forming connections with Ignite volunteers as well as other guests. We have seen this happen time and time again. Many people who started 'using' us just for food are now committed Christians, because they were allowed to move at their own pace.

Other people stay on the fringes for weeks or months, sometimes even years. But when life throws them a curve ball, when difficult things happen in their lives, they know where to come for support and often come looking for us at Ignite. Because they have experienced an unconditional and generous welcome, we have earned the right to speak into their lives and help them through whatever struggles they are having to cope with.

That, in our opinion, is God at work, to which we say a definite 'Amen'.

Reflection

How will it be for you to welcome someone unconditionally? Can you and the team set aside judgements and allow people to connect with God at their own pace and 'use' you to do this?

Prayer

Father God, thank you for reminding me how both Abraham and Jesus showed hospitality. I pray that my team and I will always do likewise, so that we will be a blessing to our guests. In Jesus' name. Amen.

13

How do we measure success?

'Blessed is the one who trusts in the Lord, whose confidence is in him. They will be like a tree planted by the water that sends out its roots by the stream. It does not fear when heat comes; its leaves are always green. It has no worries in a year of drought and never fails to bear fruit.'

JEREMIAH 17:7–8 (NIV)

Towards the end of the film *An Officer and a Gentleman*, Zack Mayo, played by Richard Gere, has just graduated from his officer training course. He walks up to his training sergeant, Emil Foley, who not only steered Mayo through some major transformations in his life but also gave him a massively hard time. After handing Foley a silver dollar – traditional payment for his 'work' – Mayo says, ' I won't ever forget you, sergeant.' Foley replies, 'I know.'

Mayo then goes on to say, 'I wouldn't have made this if it weren't for you.' Foley, visibly touched, gruffly replies, 'Get the hell out of here.'

Despite many challenges and hardships, Mayo had successfully managed to change his life, and the measurement of that success was the fact that he graduated as an 'officer and a gentleman'. Likewise, it's helpful to understand what success looks like at Ignite and how it could be measured.

Having made it this far in the book, you have probably worked out that we are not particularly strategic thinkers. On the other hand, if you are excited about measured outcomes and have skipped to this part of the book, then sadly we may have to disappoint you.

Measuring outcomes was never something we did in any structured way when we started our first Ignite. We simply saw that Ignite enabled people to hear about God more easily. Essentially, it gave them access to living water that enabled them (as the scripture quote above mentions) to lay down deep roots and grow in faith.

It was only when we were asked to replicate Ignite across Canterbury Diocese that the question of how we measure success came up. When people give you money to produce something, they want proof – tangible, measurable outcomes – that their money has been, or is being, well used. The problem, however, is that how we measure success from a Christian perspective is both a valid question and a difficult one.

We thought hard about what outcomes we could measure. There were the usual statistics when number crunching in the Church of England: attendance figures, baptisms, confirmations. Those would be easy to provide, but did they really measure success?

To highlight the problem with using baptism as a measure of success, you may have heard the joke about the three vicars having lunch together. The first vicar said, 'You know, I've been having a lot of trouble with bats in the loft and attic at my church. I've tried everything – noise, spray, cats – nothing seems to scare them away.' The second replied, 'Me too. I've got hundreds of those things living in my belfry. I had the whole place fumigated, but they still won't go away.' The third then said, 'I had that problem a while ago. So, I baptised them. Haven't seen one back since!'

Sorry, it's a terrible joke. But it highlights the concerns that we had, namely that traditional church methods of measuring success were not particularly helpful.

Next, we worked with our Ignite project board members (these were the people who provided oversight for what we were doing) to produce a theory around the change that occurs when people connect to Ignite, as shown in the following diagram.

Ignite Theory of Change

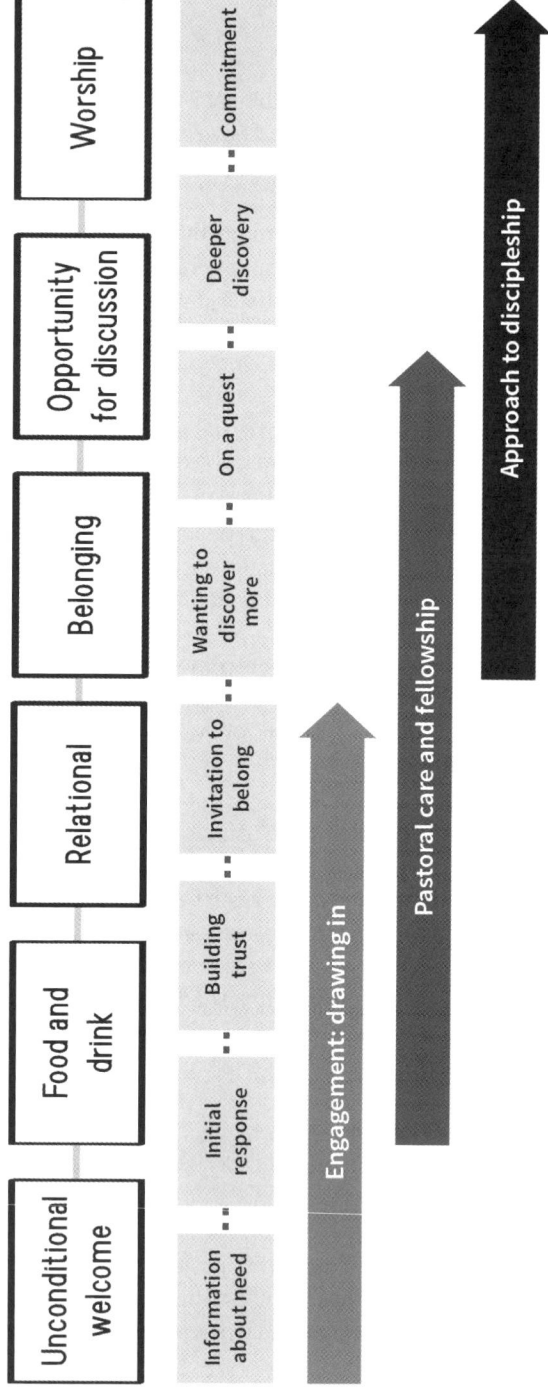

Unconditional welcome	Food and drink	Relational	Belonging	Opportunity for discussion	Worship

Information about need	Initial response	Building trust	Invitation to belong	Wanting to discover more	On a quest	Deeper discovery	Commitment

Engagement: drawing in

Pastoral care and fellowship

Approach to discipleship

The top row highlights well how Ignite helps people to connect and feel like they belong. However, although the term 'worship' at the end of the row doesn't quite fully describe an Ignite session, it does aid understanding.

The second row shows the personal engagement with people. This is the engagement that starts before they even come into church. It begins with us receiving information from someone about either a personal need or a perceived community need. This need is likely to be picked up at the point of community engagement, it shows a relational journey that is a journey of building trust and ends with commitment.

At the point of commitment some may go on to be baptised. In Cliftonville Ignite, for example, many people really valued this, especially because there was a walk-in baptistry, so they could be baptised by full immersion as a display of their faith. In other Ignite communities this transition to baptism happened much less. Perhaps this was because it depended on how involved the vicar was with Ignite. If the vicar wasn't well known by the Ignite congregation, then it was probably always going to be difficult for people to relate to a new person, when they have previously been nurtured and looked after by the Ignite team. It may also depend on whether baptisms can happen within the Ignite service or if the vicar insists on the baptism happening in the main service.

Since we strongly believe that Ignite is as valid an expression of church as the traditional Sunday service, we would always prefer to invite the 'main service' congregation to Ignite for the baptisms. Let's celebrate together!

Another way of measuring outcomes that we have used came from Michael Moynagh's discipleship statements (see *Godsend*, 2023, unit 13) and work by the Church Army (see **churcharmy.org/wp-content/uploads/2021/06/discipleship-definitions.pdf**). In the original version of the former there were seven statements; we used five (see the table on the next page).

We found this method much easier to work with. If it would be helpful, the number denoting where the Ignite member is perceived to be on their journey could periodically be placed in a column within the attendance register. This could be a helpful reminder, as often when we journey closely with people, we move with them and forget where they started from.

#	Headline statement	Possible indicators
1	**Distrustful** – I'm suspicious of the Christian faith.	– Reacts adversely to the openly religious elements of an Ignite evening – Dismissive of God and Jesus when asked questions
2	**Indifferent** – I like the Ignite community but I have no real interest in Jesus.	– Enjoys the social aspect and appears committed to it – Doesn't respond to prompts about God and Jesus
3	**Curious and open** – I'm somewhere between 'Jesus seems interesting' and 'Jesus could be for me'.	– Having loose conversations about Jesus – Asking questions about God and Jesus – Asking for prayer
4	**Actively seeking** – I want to explore following Jesus.	– Active engagement in Bible study or other learning – Deeper questioning
5	**Following and serving Jesus** – I'm actively on the journey.	– Offering to pray – Testimonies – Being prepared to help others on their journeys – Real signs of commitment – e.g. participation in non-Ignite forms of worship or playing a part in leading Ignite worship – Baptism/confirmation

Needless to say, this should never be said or done with the person – it's just for our benefit and information. After all, imagine saying to someone, 'Congratulations! You were a 2 – Indifferent – and now we see that you're a 3 – Curious and open.' You might suddenly discover you have turned them into a definite 1 – Distrustful.

We realise that a register is not something that happens in a 'normal' church service. At Ignite we record who is coming in; it would be difficult to count attendance during the evening as people move around quite a bit. We also take phone numbers if people are happy to share them. Essentially, the register enables us to contact people who we are concerned about, especially where we can see that attendance has started to decrease. A quick but caring phone call often has a real impact on people.

We quote Jeremiah 17:7–8 at the start of this chapter, as it fits with what we have often seen happen in those that we have been privileged to journey with so far. We have met many people who have little resilience to weather what life throws at them. You could say they have shallow, thirsty roots and most of their leaves are brittle and fragile. These are people who often struggle with feeling secure, and they sometimes look for security in all the wrong places – abusive or controlling relationships, alcohol, drugs and other destructive lifestyles. They can often lash out at others, mainly because they are not coping. This makes them less acceptable in mainstream society and prevents them from getting the help they need or are entitled to. Lurching from one crisis to another, they hurt themselves and others in the process.

Along the way, we have seen changes in many of those who battle with these struggles, as they start understanding how connecting with God through Jesus is relevant for them. We see people discovering a newfound valuing of themselves as human beings who are utterly loved by God. For us, this is the true measure of success. People who begin to love themselves more, love others more and even start to love God more. They have started to lay down those deeper roots and draw on the living water that we thought about earlier in this chapter.

Finally, to whet your appetite, and in thankfulness to God, we wanted to share two examples of people whose lives have been changed through their engagement with Ignite. We've changed their names to maintain their privacy.

- Julie came to Ignite before lockdown, after her children were taken into care. She was at a very low point, when the team befriended and supported her, including during lockdown. Since then, she has turned her life around. She helps at her local Ignite service every week since it reopened and regularly brings home-baked cakes. She said that without Ignite she probably wouldn't have survived the last few years, and that the Ignite team saved her life. She is now in contact with her children and looking forward to Christmas. She said she can see God's love at Ignite, and she wants to help others now.

- John is another of our amazing life-changers. He has alcohol problems and a long history with the criminal justice system. We supported him closely in the early days, and he came to Ignite most weeks, improving every time we saw him. He says that at Ignite he can be himself and be honest about his problems. One Ignite he approached a leader and said, 'You know I have some weaknesses and stuff; can you just shift that handbag that someone has left open over there please? I don't want it to be a temptation for me, if you know what I mean.' He winked and then sat down again. He is a man of great faith despite his life issues and says it's God that gives him the strength to not do bad stuff any longer.

Reflection

What does success look like from my perspective?

How will I know how well my Ignite service is doing? Am I happy using the success indicators mentioned in this chapter or do I want to try something else?

Prayer

Dear God, let me never forget that true success is a life lived in loving obedience to you. In so doing, may I successfully share the good news of Jesus with others, by being salt and light within my community. Amen.

14

Ready, steady, go!

The heart of man plans his way, but the Lord establishes his steps.
PROVERBS 16:9 (ESV)

Remembering everything that you need to do or take with you before you go on a journey can be a bit of a nightmare, as Kevin McCallister's parents, Kate and Peter, discovered in the film *Home Alone*. Sitting on the plane as it flies to Paris, not realising that Kevin was still at home, Kate rattles through a checklist with Peter, knowing she'd forgotten something but unable to remember what. Was it the coffee machine, the lights, the door? Then she suddenly remembers and, sitting bolt upright, screams, 'Kevin!'

Remembering everything you need before you launch an Ignite evening can also be tricky. So, because we are thoughtful and caring we've made you a checklist. After all, we wouldn't want you to forget Kevin.

The Ignite service checklist

Getting the business end sorted

☐ GDPR compliant

☐ public liability insurance

☐ licences for music and video clip usage

☐ food hygiene certificates, both for the premises and kitchen volunteers

☐ first aid certificates for several volunteers

☐ up-to-date first aid kit

Getting the equipment sorted

☐ projector and screen

☐ adequate sound system that can handle the various mics and audio from the projector

☐ clip-on mics x 2

☐ handheld mics x 2

☐ laptop/PC

☐ chairs and tables – our preference is Ikea coffee tables (though other coffee tables are available)

☐ photocopier

☐ laminator

Getting the 'needed every week' stuff sorted

☐ physical Ignite banner as well as social media presence, to advertise Ignite

☐ Ignite running orders (and all necessary resources)

☐ several video countdown timers

☐ prayer cards plus something to hang the cards on, such as a large wooden cross or a 'prayer tree'

☐ labels to write people's names on

☐ sweets/crisps to put out on tables

☐ sense of humour

☐ team lanyards

☐ a generous spirit

☐ storage cupboard – probably the biggest challenge in a church!

Getting the volunteers sorted

☐ up-front leaders x 2

☐ table facilitators

☐ laptop and sound desk operators

☐ cook/kitchen team

☐ welcomers (can later become table facilitators)

☐ volunteers to sign guests in (can later become table facilitators)

Reflection

There's a lot of stuff to sort out when initially launching an Ignite service. Am I the best person to do this or is there someone else who is gifted in organising things like this?

Could the organising be shared between several people?

Prayer

Dear God, here we are, me and my team, just about ready to launch our Ignite service. We have sought your will; we have tried to respond to your prompting and guidance. Now prepare us for whatever lies ahead. Regardless of how many guests turn up, may they know that they are loved and valued by both us and you. In Jesus' name. Amen.

15

Ignite service running orders

Ignite running orders are simply our service sheets. We use them for the team to prompt what we are doing next and to ensure that we stay on time.

Timing is important. It's easy to spend too much time on the games at the beginning and then either run late or end up reducing the time you spend on the other material. That's why you can see that we show both the time and how long each section will take. It's important to do both as the actual time keeps you on track when you glance at the clock, and the time allocated gives you a quick prompt as to how long each segment should be.

The schedule of an Ignite running order contains different icons to denote different types of activities. The speech icon 🔳 is used when people are sitting and listening to someone talking. The flag icon 🔳 is used when they are involved in doing something interactive. The play icon ▶ is used when we are watching something on the screen. Using icons in this way helps us to see the balance of a service. For example, if the previous Ignite service included a lot of listening activities, we may make the next session more interactive. Keep it varied and interesting.

At the start of any Ignite service you will see that we use ice-breaker questions on a rolling PowerPoint slideshow. These questions simply give things for people to chat about, to enable them to talk to each other more easily. They might have links to the theme to subliminally start people thinking in our direction of travel, but they don't need to. Questions like 'What's your favourite food?' or 'What came first – the chicken or the egg?' or 'What pet would you most like to have and why?' are simply there to act as conversation starters and create a bit of fun.

Like any church we have notices every week, but we also share encouragements with each other – what's gone well for them or other little (or big) victories they have experienced during the past week. Doing this enables people to contribute to building up the Ignite community, and it is another way of building relationships and sharing concerns. It also helps people to start vocalising their thoughts and primes them for speaking out later in the session.

To kick off the service, we always have a game, one that is invariably an Ignite version of any number of well-known TV game shows. Choose games that work for you. Some of our favourites have been hilarious versions of *Blockbusters, The Price Is Right* and *Play Your Cards Right*, to name but a few. People love to join in with these games – a live opportunity to be on a 'game show' with prizes. What's not to like?

Further resources for Ignite services can be found at **canterburydiocese.org/ mission/ignite/ignite-resources**.

MARK`S GOSPEL (EIGHT SESSIONS)

1 Introduction

Introducing the idea that the Bible is made up of many books, and that Mark's gospel is one of them.

Resources: name labels; ice-breaker PowerPoint questions; prayer labels and pens; drinks and prepared meal; video countdown timer; game resources; 'Harry Potter' quiz; first link talk; picture for *The Krypton Factor*-style quiz; second link talk; notes for ad-lib *Alas Smith and Jones*-style sketch

🚩 **7.00 pm   Doors open   30 min**

Name labels given out, tea and coffee served, ice-breaker questions on screen.

🚩 **7.30 pm   Meal   30 min**

▶️ **7.55 pm   Video countdown timer   5 min**

🚩 **8.00 pm   Game   10 min**

💬 **8.10 pm   Notices and encouragements   5 min**

🚩 **8.15 pm   Whole group activity   6 min**

Quiz on the 'Harry Potter' series of books, which links to the fact that the Bible is also comprised of a series of books, etc.

💬 **8.21 pm   Link talk   2 min**

▶️ **8.23 pm**   Video clip   2 min

Short video about seeing an event from different points of view:
youtu.be/_SsccRkLLzU

🚩 **8.25 pm**   Up-front activity 6 min

Four people look at a PowerPoint slide of a very busy picture, such as
Where's Wally or *Where's the Unicorn Now?*, for one minute. Then ask each
person to write down what they saw in the picture. You should get four
different perspectives, which will allow you to move into the next link talk.

💬 **8.31 pm**   Link talk   3 min

Explain that just like we had four different perspectives on the picture,
the gospels offer four different perspectives on Jesus. Explain that we are
going to be looking at one of those perspectives – Mark's gospel – over the
next few weeks.

▶️ **8.34 pm**   Ad-lib sketch: *Alas Smith and Jones* style   5 min

The two actors are discussing what they particularly like about Mark's
gospel. Keep it light-hearted! Actors do it ad-lib from brief notes.

💬 **8.39 pm**   Final prayer and finish   2 min

Remember to mention that there are people available to pray with and to
chat to.

💬 **8.41 pm**   End

Harry Potter quiz

1   How many Harry Potter books are there?
Seven

2   What was the title of the first book?
Harry Potter and the Philosopher's Stone

3   Who wrote the Harry Potter series?
J.K. Rowling

4   What sport does Harry Potter play?
Quidditch

5   What was the name of the last book?
Harry Potter and the Deathly Hallows

6   Who was Harry's arch enemy?
Lord Voldemort

7   Which school house did Harry belong to?
Gryffindor

8   We've already had the titles of two Harry Potter books. Now name the other five.
Harry Potter and the... Chamber of Secrets; Prisoner of Azkaban; Goblet of Fire; Order of the Phoenix; Half-blood Prince

9   Why are there eight Harry Potter films?
Because the last book was made into two films

10   What is a muggle?
A muggle is a person who lacks any sort of magical ability and was not born into the magical world

2 John the Baptist

MARK 1:1–8

Resources: name labels; ice-breaker PowerPoint questions; prayer labels and pens; drinks and cakes/doughnuts; video countdown timer; game resources; eating weird food video; weird food to eat during activity; John the Baptist film clip; John the Baptist quiz; prepared talk; Delirious? video song

🏳 **7.00 pm   Doors open   30 min**

Name labels given out, prayer labels and pens distributed around tables, drinks and cakes/doughnuts served, ice-breaker questions on screen.

▶ **7.25 pm   Video countdown timer   5 min**

🏳 **7.30 pm   Game   10 min**

💬 **7.40 pm   Notices and encouragements   5 min**

▶ **7.45 pm   Video clip   3 min**

A video clip about eating weird food, like ants: **youtu.be/JxE_iuDWBbo**

🏳 **7.48 pm   Up-front activity 10 min**

Invite some guests to come up and try some weird insect food! These can be bought beforehand online.

🏳 **7.58 pm   Whole group activity   4 min**

Take the mic around guests and ask them to guess who we are thinking about.

▶ 8.02 pm   Video clip   4 min

A video clip about John the Baptist: **youtu.be/F-MDVv6Yaf0**

⚑ 8:06 pm   Whole group activity   10 min

A quiz on John the Baptist. *Note: you will need to create your own John the Baptist quiz.*

💬 8.16 pm   Talk   5 min

▶ 8.21 pm   Video song   4 min

'Did You Feel the Mountains Tremble?' by Delirious?:
youtu.be/ek26sskZERQ

💬 8:25 pm   Final prayer and finish   2 min

Remember to mention that there are people available to pray with and to chat to.

💬 8.28 pm   End

3 Spending time with Jesus is good for us

MARK 2:13–17

Resources: name labels; ice-breaker PowerPoint questions; prayer labels and pens; drinks and prepared meal; video countdown timer; game resources; bandages; scripture reading on PowerPoint; printed cut-up scripture verses from the reading, sufficient for each table; prepared talk; video song

🏳 7.00 pm   Doors open   30 min

Name labels given out, prayer labels and pens distributed around tables, tea and coffee served, icebreaker questions on screen.

🏳 7.30 pm   Meal   30 min

▶ 7.55 pm   Countdown video   5 min

🏳 8.00 pm   Game   10 min

💬 8.10 pm   Notices and encouragements   5 min

🏳 8.15 pm   Up-front activity   8 min

Get three pairs of people up front and have one person from each pair put a bandage on the second person in the pair. Get the person being bandaged to over-act feeling poorly with moans and groans before being bandaged, and then to sound happier after being bandaged.

8.23 pm   Link   2 min

Explain that just like the people who were poorly were made to feel better by the people who bandaged them up, Jesus can make us feel better by spending time with him.

8.25 pm   Scripture reading   2 min

Put up the PowerPoint scripture reading.

8.27 pm   Table group activity   8 min

Give each table group the reading, which has already been cut out into separate verses. Ask people to decide which are positive verses and which are negative – which verses are talking about something that is good, and which are talking about something that is not so good. Also, some of the verses may just be a statement and are therefore neither positive nor negative. They must decide. Then get feedback from the table groups.

8.35 pm   Talk   5 min

Explain that spending time with Jesus is good for us and makes us feel better about ourselves. Explain that we can spend time with Jesus through praying, reading the Bible, going to church and mixing with other Christians.

8.40 pm   Video song   4 min

'Shake' by MercyMe: **youtu.be/YJFA5Bitv7w**

8.44 pm   Finish   2 min

Remember to mention that there are people available to pray with and to chat to.

8.46 pm   End

Points you may want to include

You may want to include the following points in the talk:

- Premise – Just being in Jesus' presence makes us feel better about ourselves.
- Jesus' birth – 'I bring you good news that will cause great joy for all the people' (Luke 2:10, NIV).
- Jesus wants his joy to be in us so that our joy can be complete (see John 15:11).
- Wedding at Cana (John 2:1–10).
- Calling of Levi and eating with sinners (Mark 2:13–17).
- Samaritan woman (John 4:1–30) – 'Come, see a man who told me everything I've ever done' (v. 29, NIV).
- Jesus positively affected/transformed the lives of all these and many more: Bartimaeus; lepers; the ill; the depressed; a woman with bleeding; the dead!
- How do we spend quality time in Jesus' presence? Through praying, reading scripture, worshipping, going to church, mixing with other Christians and so on.

4 We are measured by the same measure that we use against others

MARK 4:24

Resources: name labels; ice-breaker PowerPoint questions; prayer labels and pens; drinks and cakes/doughnuts; video countdown timer; game resources; Smarties; bowls; different sized measures; Mark 4:24 sketch; A1 cards and craft materials

7.00 pm   Doors open   30 min

Name labels given out, prayer labels and pens distributed around tables, drinks and cakes/doughnuts served, ice-breaker questions on screen.

7.25 pm   Video countdown timer   5 min

7.30 pm   Game   10 min

7.40 pm   Notices and encouragements   5 min

7.45 pm   Up-front activity 8 min

Three people are invited up to the front and are each given a bowl of Smarties. They choose from one of four different measures to give away sweets. Although they are not told what will happen, they are given some sweets themselves based on the measure that they have given.

7.53 pm   Sketch   5 min

Sketch based on Mark 4:24 (see below).

7.58 pm   Link talk   2 min

Explain that how we measure (judge, accept) people, affects how we ourselves are measured, judged and accepted by others.

8:00 pm   Whole group activity   10 min

This activity is called the Yes, No, Maybe game. People have to choose one
of those three answers to certain questions. The questions are: (1) Should
we let refugees into the country? (2) If you found someone's wallet, filled
with money and credit cards, would you hand it in to the police? (3) If you
saw someone being bullied on the bus, would you say or do something?
Use people's answers to facilitate a whole-group discussion.

8.10 pm   Link talk   3 min

This is where we link the positive outworking of Mark 4:24 with John 15:12:
'Love each other as I have loved you' (NIV).

8.13 pm   Table group activity   15 min

Four groups each decorate their own A1-sized piece of card, using the
words of John 15:12 as their theme. However, we found that it was helpful
to have a prayer card response available for those who either don't want
to do the craft activity or for people to fill out while doing the craft activity. This enables people to pray for those who they have measured too
harshly. *Note: you will need to create your own prayer card.*

8:28 pm   Finish   2 min

Remember to mention that there are people available to pray with and
chat to.

8.30 pm   End

Mark 4:24 sketch

Characters: Mr Smith; Delivery man (DM); Bag; Narrator

Props: flat cap for the delivery driver; clipboard; three plain bags that look full (it doesn't matter with what, as the contents won't be seen) and loosely tied.

Notes: both the Bag and the Narrator's lines need to be said off-stage via a mic. These can be done by the same person.

DM	Ding-dong!
Mr Smith	Oh, hello.
DM	Alright, mate? Got a special delivery. You Mr Smith?
Mr Smith	Yes, that's me.
DM	Right. Sign 'ere then, please.
Mr Smith	Who's it from?
DM	*(Looks at the clipboard.)* It says 'ere that it's from a Mister – can't quite make out the name – a Mister J. Hoover or Mister J. Hova, or something like that. Well, at least that's what it says 'ere!
Mr Smith	But what is it?
DM	Well I don't know, do I? Why don't you open one of them bags and found out?
Mr Smith	Good idea. I'll open this one. Oh, look, it's got a label on it. It says, 'Judging' – that's a bit weird! Still, here goes!

Mr Smith begins to open the bag. From the bag comes a 'voice', really criticising and judging Mr Smith.

Bag Can't you do anything right? You just make a mess of even the simplest thing! I can't even trust you to feed the dog without spilling dog biscuits everywhere! In fact, if I left the dog to feed himself there would be less mess. At least he'd clear up the stuff on the floor. You are as much use as a chocolate teapot!

Mr Smith quickly reties the bag.

DM Now that really *was* weird!

Mr Smith Not half! Do you suppose they're all like that?

DM I dunno mate. Try another one and find out.

Mr Smith Er... Okay... I suppose...

Mr Smith begins to untie another bag. This time the voice is scathing and unaccepting.

Bag You are rubbish! Do you know that? You are a menace to society, an absolute waste of space, an air thief! I don't know why I bother with you at all. You are nothing, and will always be nothing! I didn't like you when I met you, and I still don't like you!

Mr Smith That's horrible! Surely, they can't all be like this?

DM *(Picks up another bag and holds it up to his ear.)* Blimey, this one sounds really cross. *(Looks at the label.)* Oh, that explains it. It says 'Impatience'.

Mr Smith But... but... why have they been sent to me?

DM Let me look at me delivery notes for you. *(Consults his clipboard.)* Erm, it says... it's the same as what you've given out to lots of other people, so Mr Hova thought it was only fair that he gave the same amount back to you.

Mr Smith But what am I supposed to do with all of this?

DM	Not my department, mate, sorry! I just do the deliveries… Anyway, give us a moment and I'll bring in the rest.
Mr Smith	The rest?
DM	Oh yeah, didn't I say? I've got another two thousand of these bags outside, waiting to be brought in.
Mr Smith	Two thousand?!
DM	Yeah, but don't worry; the others are coming tomorrow!
Narrator	And God's word says, the way you treat others will be the way you will be treated – and even worse!

End

5 How do we respond to authority?

MARK 4:35–41

Resources: name labels; ice-breaker PowerPoint questions; prayer labels and pens; drinks and prepared meal; video countdown timer; game resources; pictures for the authority activity; scripture reading on PowerPoint; prepared talk

7.00 pm   Doors open   30 min

Name labels given out, prayer labels distributed around tables, tea and coffee served, ice-breaker questions on screen.

7.30 pm   Meal   30 min

7.55 pm   Video countdown timer   5 min

8.00pm   Game   10 min

8.10 pm   Notices and encouragements   5 min

8.15 pm   Up-front activity 6 min

For this activity, you will need A4-size printed pictures of: a teacher; a police officer; a vicar; a doctor; a judge; an RSPCA officer; a bailiff; the current prime minister; a community care support worker. Get enough people to come up and hold a picture each, for the rest of the congregation to see. (*Note: if your congregation isn't that big, reduce the number of pictures. Just be sure to include some contentious ones for a lively discussion!*) Ask the congregation to put pictures in order of those who have the most authority.

8.21 pm   Whole congregation discussion   2 min

Why do we need authority? *Note: authority is good if it used in the right way. Whether we like it or not, someone has generally got authority over us.*

8.23 pm   Scripture reading   2 min

8.25 pm   Table group discussion   8 min

How much authority do we believe Jesus has? Does Jesus have authority now? Then get people to feed back their answers.

8.33 pm   Talk   5 min

8.38 pm   Finish   2 min

Remember to mention that there are people available to pray with and to chat to.

8.40 pm   End

6 You can do a lot with very little

MARK 6:6b–13

Resources: name labels; ice-breaker PowerPoint questions; prayer labels and pens; drinks and cakes/doughnuts; video countdown timer; game resources; two dozen eggs and two egg trays; Eddie the Eagle video clip; info guide about Eddie the Eagle; 'Bare minimum' list; scripture PowerPoint; Nick Vujicic video clip

7.00 pm   Doors open   30 min

Name labels given out, prayer labels and pens distributed around tables, drinks and cakes/doughnuts served, ice-breaker questions on screen.

7.25 pm   Video countdown timer   5 min

7.30 pm   Game   10 min

7.40 pm   Notices and encouragements   5 min

7.45 pm   Up-front activity 8 min

Use a team member or a volunteer to stand on the eggs – it can be done, honest! This is to show that something small (e.g. eggs) can do/support something big: you can do a lot with very little!

7.53 pm   Link talk   3 min

How can we do lots/great things with simple things/a small amount?

▶   7.56 pm   Video clip   3 min

A video clip about Eddie the Eagle: **youtu.be/L1aWsFpg3To**

🎞️   7.59 pm   Info guide to Eddie the Eagle   5 min

Give the congregation some stats and interesting facts about how Eddie the Eagle managed to take part in the Olympics. Again, comment that he achieved great things with very little.

🚩   8.04 pm   Table group activity   10 min

Give each table group a suggested list of necessities for a happy life. Groups have to choose five items from the list – the bare minimum – to give them a happy life, then feed back their answers.

🎞️   8.14 pm   Scripture reading followed by link talk   4 min

Mark 6:6b–13. Link talk to explain the scripture. Try not to use too much Christian jargon when explaining it.

▶   8:18 pm   Video clip   5 min

Nick Vujicic, born without any arms and legs, shows that much can be done with very little: **youtu.be/6F8zK57Wa0A**

🎞️   8.23 pm   Sum up the evening   3 min

🎞️   8.26 pm   Finish   2 min

Remember to mention that there are people available to pray with and to chat to.

🎞️   8.28 pm   End

The 'bare minimum' list

Regular income
Friendship
Clothes
Job
Family
House
Food
Car
50" top spec TV
Faith
Church
Good health
Love
Husband/wife/partner
Pet
Yearly holiday
Responsibility
Credit card
Respect
Good career prospects
Something else?

Your five choices

1 _____

2 _____

3 _____

4 _____

5 _____

7 God can do the impossible

MARK 6:30-44

Resources: name labels; ice-breaker PowerPoint questions; prayer labels and pens; drinks and prepared meal; video countdown timer; game resources; A4 paper, A4 example; monologue based on Mark 6:30–44; prepared talk; printed prayer response cards

🚩 7.00 pm Doors open 30 min

Name labels given out, prayer labels distributed around tables, tea and coffee served, ice-breaker questions on screen.

🚩 7.30 pm Meal 30 min

▶ 7.55 pm Video countdown timer 5 min

🚩 8.00 pm Game 10 min

💬 8.10 pm Notices and encouragements 5 min

🚩 8.15 pm Table group activity 8 min

Leader's information: look at **youtu.be/8y9i8ag2WTk** for instructions on how to do this.
To introduce the theme of not everything that seems impossible *is* impossible, hand out a sheet of A4 paper and a pair of scissors to each table group and ask them to create a hole in the paper which they can step through. After five or six minutes, show them how it's done.

8.23 pm   Link talk   2 min

God can take what looks like impossible and make it possible – because he's God!

8.25 pm   Monologue   4 min

Humorous monologue, based on the feeding of the 5,000.

8.29 pm   Talk   5 min

8.34 pm   Prayer response 6 min

Give each table group some blank A6 prayer-response cards. Our card had a simple line drawing of bread and fish on the front of the card, to remind people of the feeding of the 5,000. Invite everyone, if they want to, to write a short prayer request on the card and then bring it up to the front, perhaps putting it in a basket or laying it at the foot of a cross. Remind the congregation that nothing is impossible with God.

8.40 pm   Prayer for the response requests   2 min

8.42 pm   Finish   2 min

Remember to mention that there are people available to pray with and to chat to.

8.44 pm   End

Not a camel burger in sight! A monologue based on Mark 6:30–44

This was originally read out in a northern accent. Pace this – don't read it too fast!

What a day. What an amazing day. One I'm not likely to forget, I can tell you! The things I've heard! And the things I've seen! You wouldn't believe it.

You know, everyone's gone now, following that Jesus again, I shouldn't wonder. But you should have been 'ere a couple of hours ago. The whole place was packed tight, right down to the bottom of the hill! There were thousands of us. At least five thousand, and that's only counting the blokes. There were women and children, even babes in arms. Whole families. That's right, whole families who'd come to listen to this Jesus bloke. Followed him for miles, they had, right out of town and up into the hills.

Well, before you could even say, 'Oy vey, my son,' it was teatime, and not a McDonalds or a Camel Burger King in sight! You see, 'ardly anyone had brought anything to eat. Well, stands to reason, dunnit? No one had expected to be traipsing round the hills at that time of day.

I'll tell you what, though; you know what kids and blokes are like when they're hungry? There was whinging and complaining, and all sorts! And those mates of Jesus, his… er… disciples, well, fat lot a good they were. They just wanted us to push off back home!

But Jesus… he was something different. He was a real gent! You know, like he really cared about us. 'They don't need to go away,' he said. And then, cool as a cucumber, he said, 'You give 'em something to eat.'

Well, 'cause I'd had the common sense to bring a bit of food with us, you know some bread and fish, and then given it to my lad to look after, the disciples grabs me lad, nicks the basket off him and says, 'But master, we've only got five loaves of bread and two fishes.' If I'd've had time, I would've been proper narked!

But that's when it 'appened. The miracle! As I live and breathe, an honest-to-God miracle.

Jesus... well... he sort of took the basket of food, thanked God for it, and then he thanked God for all the people and for the world... He said it like he really meant it...

Then, he broke the bread in half, and told the disciples to go and feed everyone. Well, that's when I thought Jesus had lost it. 'Aye-aye,' I says to me self. 'Old Jesus has had a touch too much of the sun,' if you know what I mean. *(Make a 'going crazy' gesture.)*

But I was wrong. They *did feed* everyone! As fast as they emptied that basket, it filled up again. And again, and again. Until everyone, from the biggest bloke to the littlest kid, had stuffed themselves stupid. In fact, if they were anything like our lad, it was probably the kids who stuffed themselves the most. *(Pause)*

Well... you know what kids are like, when there's good food about. They don't want to be left out, and they can't leave it alone, can they? I tell you what, though, my belly had never felt so full. *(Chuckles)* And I've got a big belly!

And when it was over, when everyone had left, we still had so much food we could've filled another twelve baskets! It was amazing. A real proper miracle, just like I said.

No one, not one person, got left out. It was like Jesus made everyone welcome. Didn't matter whether you were big or small, didn't matter whether you were a bloke, a woman or even a kid. Everyone got fed on just a few loaves of bread and some fish.

And all because of that Jesus.

Amazing, just amazing!

He'll go far, that Jesus will. You mark my words...

End

8 Blind Bartimaeus

MARK 10:46–52

Resources: name labels; ice-breaker PowerPoint questions; prayer labels and pens; drinks and cakes/doughnuts; video countdown timer; game resources; flipchart and paper; blindfold; prepared simple drawings; *Rogue One* blind man fight scene video clip; printed copies of scripture reading PowerPoint and scripture reading; 'Amazing Grace (My Chains Are Gone)' video song

🚩 **7.00 pm   Doors open   30 min**

Name labels given out, prayer labels and pens distributed around tables, drinks and cakes/doughnuts served, ice-breaker questions on screen.

▶ **7.25 pm   Video countdown timer   5 min**

🚩 **7.30 pm   Game   10 min**

📺 **7.40 pm   Notices and encouragements   5 min**

🚩 **7.45 pm   Up-front activity 8 min**

Ask two people to volunteer. The first person is given a simple picture, and the second person is blindfolded. The first person describes the picture and gives instructions to the second person, so they can draw it on a flipchart.

🚩 **7.53 pm   Table group activity   7 min**

Get table groups to talk about what it would be like to be blind. What would their greatest fears be? What would their greatest challenges be? Then get them to feed back.

▶ **8.00 pm**   Video clip   2 min

The blind man fight scene from the film *Rogue One*:
youtu.be/1QvpUvjCeP0

💬 **8.02 pm**   Link talk   2 min

Refer to the determination and ability of the blind fighter, and then mention that there was also another man who was blind who also had a high level of determination – Blind Bartimaeus.

▶ **8.04 pm**   Scripture reading from Mark 10:46–52   2 min

Put up the PowerPoint scripture reading and read this out loud.

🚩 **8.06 pm**   Table discussion 7 min

Give each table group a printed copy of the reading and ask them to look at it. What things do people find interesting about the reading? Or odd? Or difficult to understand? Then get people to feed back their thoughts.

💬 **8.13 pm**   Talk   5 min

▶ **8.18 pm**   Video song   4 min

'Amazing Grace (My Chains Are Gone)': **youtu.be/Jbe7OruLk8I**

💬 **8.22 pm**   Final prayer and finish   2 min

Remember to mention that there are people available to pray with and to chat to.

💬 **8.24 pm**   End

Notes for the talk

Bartimaeus was determined! He wouldn't give up. Despite people telling him to be quiet, Bartimaeus was determined to have an encounter with Jesus. As a result, his life is transformed.

Don't let anyone stop you from have a life changing encounter with Jesus.

Bartimaeus got rid of his cloak, maybe because he didn't want to trip up, or perhaps he didn't want any material possessions to come between him and Jesus.

Imagine throwing everything of value you own aside – your car, your phone or your TV – to get closer to Jesus.

Jesus asked Bartimaeus what seems like a silly question: 'What do you want me to do for you?' Jesus knew exactly what he needed. But he wanted Bartimaeus to spell it out for him, because he wanted Bartimaeus to trust him.

Let's not sell ourselves short in our prayer requests. We need to be honest with God and spell out what we really need.

We are told in the Bible reading that when Jesus gave Bartimaeus his sight, Bartimaeus 'followed Jesus along the road.'

Perhaps today, we need to be brave and invite Jesus into our lives and become one of his followers.

FRIENDSHIP (TWO SESSIONS)

These sessions were written at a time when there were issues with friendships within Ignite. They were helpful in addressing issues and showing how Jesus can be our most trusted friend.

1 Friendship with others

PROVERBS 18:24

Resources: name labels; ice-breaker PowerPoint questions; prayer labels and pens; drinks and cakes/doughnuts; video countdown timer; game resources; *Toy Story* video song; friendship sayings on PowerPoint and on paper; *Men Behaving Badly* video clip; foam dice with friendship attributes attached; prayer cards; lengths of string to tie round wrists; empty display board; songs from James Taylor and Queen

7.00 pm   Doors open   30 min

Name labels given out, prayer labels and pens distributed around tables, drinks and cakes/doughnuts served, ice-breaker questions on screen.

7.25 pm   Video countdown timer   5 min

7.30 pm   Game   10 min

7.40 pm   Notices and encouragements   5 min

Mention prayer labels for people to write their prayers on and hang on a prayer tree, cross etc. and that all prayers will be prayed at the next Sunday service.

7.45 pm   Video song   5 min

'You've got a friend in me' from *Toy Story*: **youtu.be/ZjbSKknc2rc**

7.50 pm   Link   2 min

Introducing the theme of friendship.

■ **7.52 pm   Table group activity   10 min**

Note: You can find lots of quotes about friendship – both good and awful – online. Show a selection of friendship sayings on a PowerPoint slide and ask for either the 'Ah' or the 'Vomit' factor! Then distribute some more sayings that are on paper, for table groups to discuss and then feed back.

▶ **8.02 pm   Video clip   4 min**

'Tony gets glasses' from *Men Behaving Badly*: **youtu.be/tmO25vFI9cY**

■ **8.06 pm   Link talk   3 min**

Explain that just like the video showed, friendship is not always plain sailing. Friendships can sometimes be challenging. So how do we work out what real friendship is?

■ **8.09 pm   Table group activity   12 min**

A foam cube, with six different friendship qualities (some positive and some ambiguous) attached to each side, is rolled by a leader up front and then whichever attribute is facing upwards is discussed by the table groups. Briefly get their feedback after each time. *Note: You will have to buy the foam cube or you can make your own. It needs to be approximately 8 inches square.* **Only discuss three of the attributes.**

■ **8.21 pm   Interactive prayer activity   8 min**

Distribute prayer cards to table groups and invite people to add a prayer for their friend or friends. Explain that in the prayer – without writing down names – we are praying a blessing on our friends, praying something good for them. Then have people bring up their cards to the display board to pin up. As people return to their seats, they are given a piece of string to tie one or several knots in, to remember to keep praying for their friends. *Note: you will need to make and photocopy a simple prayer card.*

During prayer activity, play the following music, or other similar themed music of your choice:

- 'You've Got a Friend' by James Taylor: **youtu.be/xEkIou3WFnM**
- 'You're My Best Friend' by Queen: **youtu.be/tN_HVup9oOg**

8.29 pm   **Final prayer and finish**   2 min

Finish by praying a collective prayer of thanks for our friends.

8.31 pm   **End**

2 Jesus is the best of friends

JOHN 15:15

Resources: name labels; ice-breaker PowerPoint questions; prayer labels and pens; drinks and prepared meal; video countdown timer; game resources; A4 paper and pens for the 'Build a friendship' activity and flipchart paper; scripture references for the 'Jesus scripture hunt' activity, along with pens and paper; prepared link talk; video song and laminates for prayer response

7 00 pm   Doors open   30 min

Name labels given out, prayer labels and pens distributed around tables, drinks served, ice-breaker questions on screen.

7.30 pm   Meal   25 min

7.55 pm   Video countdown timer   5 min

8.00 pm   Game   10 min

8.10 pm   Notices and encouragements   5 min

Mention prayer labels for people to write their prayers on and hang on a prayer tree, cross, etc. and that all prayers will be prayed at the next Sunday service.

8.15 pm   Table group activity   12 min

Each table group is given an A4 sheet of paper. The first person writes at the top of the sheet one quality they think is important for a friend to have. They then fold over the paper so it can't be seen and pass it to the next person, who writes their important quality and then likewise folds over the paper and passes it on to the next person, and so on. Once the whole group has written down their different qualities, they then feed back so that we build a list of the 'ideal' friend. Write the list on one half of flipchart paper.

🚩 **8.27 pm Table group activity   12 min**

Stick up around the church different scriptures relating to different ways that Jesus shows his friendship. People go around and decide what quality that scripture shows us about Jesus being a friend. They write it down and then feed back later. During feedback, put Jesus' friendship qualities up on the other half of flip hart paper, so we can compare it to the previous list of 'ideal friend' qualities.

💬 **8.39 pm Link talk   3 min**

Compare the two lists and make the point that our first 'ideal friend' qualities list is just that – it's ideal! But not all friends are like that, and even the very best friends can still let us down. Jesus, however, never lets us down and is utterly dependable and trustworthy.

▶ **8.42 pm Prayer response 4 min**

Invite people to ask Jesus into their lives to be their friend. Do this by asking them to come up to the front, to be prayed for very simply and to take away with them a laminated prayer. As people come up, play the video song 'What a Friend I've Found' by Hillsong and Delirious?:
youtu.be/WP0LcrQzkfo

💬 **8.46 pm Finish   2 min**

As people leave, mention anything relevant to next week, that prayer and chat is available, etc.

💬 **8.48 pm End**

Suggested verses to put around the church

Notes for leaders in italics. Unless noted, the verses are our paraphrase.

1   'Greater love has no one than this, that someone lay down his life for his friends' (John 15:13, ESV). *This shows that Jesus' friendship is sacrificial.*

2   'Come to me, all who struggle and are weighed down by life, and I will give you rest' (Matthew 11:28). *This shows that as a friend, Jesus wants to help make our lives easier.*

3   'A new commandment I give to you, that you love one another: just as I have loved you, you also are to love one another' (John 13:34, ESV). *This shows that Jesus' friendship is loving.*

4   The Pharisees and the scribes grumbled, saying, 'This man [Jesus] mixes with sinners and even eats with them' (Luke 15:2). *This shows that Jesus' friendship is for everyone.*

5   On the third day a wedding took place at Cana in Galilee... Jesus and his friends were also there' (John 2:1–2). *This shows that Jesus liked to live life and celebrate life with his friends.*

6   As he was being crucified, Jesus said, 'Father, forgive them, because they don't know what they are doing' (Luke 23:34). *This shows that Jesus' friendship towards us involves unconditional forgiveness.*

7   Then Jesus said to them, 'My soul is overwhelmed, to the point of death; stay here and keep me company' (Matthew 26:38). *This shows that Jesus' friendship involved him opening up and being real and honest with his friends.*

8   Jesus said, 'I have compassion on these people; they have already been with me three days and have nothing to eat. If I send them home hungry, they will collapse on the way' (Mark 8:2–3). *This shows that Jesus' friendship is filled with compassion. He fed them.*

9   'Peace I leave with you; my peace I give to you' (John 14:27, ESV). *This shows that Jesus' friendship is good for us! It brings us peace.*

10 On the beach, Jesus said to Peter and the others, 'Come and have breakfast'… Jesus took the bread and gave it to them and did the same with the fish (John 21:12–13). *You might need to explain the context of this verse. It comes in the aftermath of Peter having denied three times his friendship with Jesus. This verse shows that Jesus' friendship forgives and doesn't hold any grudges when we fail.*

Suggested words for a prayer laminate

Lord Jesus, I need your love and friendship in my life. Thank you for dying on the cross to pay the price for the things that I have done wrong. Please forgive me and help me to live a new life with you as my Lord, Friend and Saviour. Thank you, Jesus. Amen.

THE TRINITY (FOUR SESSIONS)

This series aims to introduce a complex idea in a way that allows people to begin to understand the nature of God – Father, Son and Holy Spirit. You will see that there is repetition within these sessions as we try to connect them together within people's thinking.

![1] Introduction to the holy Trinity

Resources: name labels; ice-breaker PowerPoint questions; prayer labels and pens; drinks and cakes/doughnuts; video countdown timer; game resources; activity sheets with objects or words to be put into groups of three; strips of paper (2" x A4 width); prepared display board showing the word 'God' in the centre, then having three sections labelled 'Father', 'Jesus' and 'Holy Spirit'; holy Trinity video clip.

🚩 **7.00 pm   Doors open   30 min**

Name labels given out, prayer labels and pens distributed around tables, drinks and cakes/doughnuts served, ice-breaker questions on screen.

▶️ **7.25 pm   Video countdown timer   5 min**

🚩 **7.30 pm   Game   10 min**

💬 **7.40 pm   Notices and encouragements   5 min**

🚩 **7.45 pm   Table activity   8 min**

Each table group are given a list of words that they need to put into groups of three – e.g. bush, plant, tree; water, steam, ice; car, bus, train. Make them as hard or easy as you think your group will need and include Father, Jesus and Holy Spirit.

💬 **7.53 pm   Link talk   5 min**

Have members try to guess the theme. Say something like: *'We are starting a new series looking at the holy Trinity. This is important for Christians but is also sometimes a bit of a challenge for people to get their heads round.*

So, since Christians believe that God is one being who is three different persons – told you it was a bit of a challenge – we thought we would start by first thinking about what we know about God.'

🚩 **7.58 pm   Table group activity   8 min**

Each table group are given eight or nine pre-cut strips of paper (about 2" x A4 width). Ask people to discuss what they think they know about God – what is he like and what does he do? Get them to record their findings on the strips of paper; e.g. if someone says that God is kind, they should write the word 'kind' on one of the paper strips. Then get feedback.

🚩 **8.06 pm   Table group activity   8 min**

Draw people's attention to a display board that has already been divided into three (labelled 'Father', 'Jesus', 'Holy Spirit'), with the word 'God' pinned to the centre of the board. Going to each table in turn, ask them to take up one of their answers from the previous activity and pin it in whichever section they think that answer belongs in; e.g. if the answer was 'guide', then they might want to pin it in the 'Holy Spirit' section. Then get feedback.

▶ **8.14 pm   Video clip   5 min**

Show a short video explaining the Trinity: **youtu.be/cgu2iNZHyEo**

💬 **8.19 pm   Link   4 min**

Very briefly summarise the video's three main Trinity examples and see if we can put them on the Trinity display board.

💬 **8.23 pm   Final prayer and finish   2 min**

💬 **8.25 pm   End**

2 God the Father

ISAIAH 63:16

Resources: name labels; ice-breaker PowerPoint questions; prayer labels and pens; drinks and prepared meal; video countdown timer; game resources; *Some Mothers Do 'Ave 'Em* video clip; human dads suggestion sheet; 'Father's love letter' video clip.

7.00 pm   Doors open   30 min

Name labels given out, prayer labels and pens distributed around tables, drinks served, ice-breaker questions on screen.

7.30 pm   Meal   30 min

7.55 pm   Video countdown timer   5 min

8.00 pm   Game   10 min

8.10 pm   Notices and encouragements   5 min

8.15 pm   Whole group activity   5 min

What can people remember about the previous week? Recap where necessary.

8.20 pm   Video clip   4 min

Some Mothers Do 'Ave 'Em video clip about Frank Spencer being a bumbling dad: **youtu.be/V-HfGzEkB1g**

8.24 pm   Table group activity   8 min

What are human dads like? Good and bad points? Give each table group a sheet with suggestions of what human dads can be like. Ask people to share what they think. Then get feedback.

8.32 pm   Link talk   3 min

Talk about the fact that human dads can be a mixed bunch. Like our video, some dads are well-intentioned, but still mess up. Some are not very good, kind or loving. Some human dads are amazing and brilliant. And some are mixture of all three. However, God the Father is always loving, kind and amazing. And we know this because of what we can learn about him from the Bible.

8.35 pm   Video clip   6 min

'Father's love letter': **youtu.be/zJvqmhGs1Y8**

8.41 pm   Sum up, final prayer and finish   2 min

Be aware that the previous video is very powerful and that God may create 'a moment' that needs to be prayed into. Be sensitive to the Holy Spirit moving in people.

8.42 pm   End

3 Jesus, God the Son

JOHN 15:14–17

Resources: name labels; ice-breaker PowerPoint questions; prayer labels and pens; drinks and cakes/doughnuts; video countdown timer; game resources; two Ignite team members to be the 'boffins' (experts), prepped in advance with the question; activities resources; 'Footprints' video song by Leona Lewis; laminated bookmarks showing images of footprints.

7.00 pm   Doors open   30 min

Name labels given out, prayer labels and pens distributed around tables, drinks and cakes/doughnuts served, ice-breaker questions on screen.

7.25 pm   Video countdown timer   5 min

7.30 pm   Game   10 min

7.40 pm   Notices and encouragements   5 min

7.45 pm   Whole group activity   6 min

What can people remember from last week? Recap where necessary.

7.51 pm   Table group activity   6 min

Scripture reading from John 15:14–17, then ask the following: 'Are we friends with Jesus, and if so, how is Jesus our friend?' Ask the table groups to discuss and then feed back answers.

▶ **7.57 pm   Boffins   7 min**

Question: how did you strengthen/deepen your friendship with Jesus?

⚑ **8.03 pm   Connecting with Jesus activities   10 min**

These are sort of prayer stations. Invite guests to go to one, some or all the activities, depending on the time available:
1 watching worship videos
2 lighting a candle and being quiet
3 listening to a testimony (either live or video clip)
4 decorating little wooden crosses (these can be purchased online)

⚑ **8.13 pm   Led from the front discussion   5 min**

Get feedback from people who have done the activities, asking, 'How was it for you?'

▶ **8.18 pm   Video song   4 min**

Video song based on the famous 'Footprints' poem: **youtu.be/ FabyQcmzfCM**

💬 **8.22 pm   Sum-up, final prayer and finish   2 min**

Hand out prepared laminated bookmarks as people leave.

💬 **8.24 pm   End**

4 God the Holy Spirit

JOHN 14:26

Resources: name labels; ice-breaker PowerPoint questions; prayer labels and pens; drinks and prepared meal; video countdown timer; game resources; PowerPoint scripture verse; 'Douglas' video clip and whiteboard or flipchart; Holy Spirit word search; 'Welcome Holy Spirit' video song

7.00 pm   Doors open   30 min

Name labels given out, prayer labels and pens distributed around tables, drinks served, ice-breaker questions on screen

7.30 pm   Meal   30 min

7.55 pm   Video countdown timer   5 min

8.00 pm   Game   10 min

8.10 pm   Notices and encouragements   5 min

8.15 pm   Whole group activity   5 min

What can people remember from last week? Recap where necessary. Finish with mentioning that we are finishing our series today by looking at the Holy Spirit. (Put up PowerPoint scripture verse) and read out. Then lead directly into next segment.

8.20 pm   Table group activity   6 min

What is the Holy Spirit? *Note: the question is worded this way to see if anyone says that the Holy Spirit is a 'who' and not a 'what', which is what the following 'Douglas' video clip will address.* Get feedback and write answers on to a whiteboard or flipchart.

8.26 pm   Video clip   2 min

Douglas talks about the Holy Spirit. *Note: this video is obviously aimed at children, so ham it up!* Use the previous table discussion answers to compare with what was said in the video. Remember that you only need to use the first 90–120 seconds of the video: **youtu.be/b9yN5VcHTQ0**

8.28 pm   Individual activity   5 min

Ask each person to do a word search describing the characteristics and benefits of the Holy Spirit. These can easily be created for free online.

8.33 pm   Table group activity   5 min

Encourage people to discuss their own experiences of the Holy Spirit. Be aware that some people may not even be aware that they have encountered the Holy Spirit. Get feedback.

8.38 pm   Recap talk   4 min

Recap the three things that we've learned today: Holy Spirit is a 'who' not a 'what'; when we say 'yes' to Jesus, he comes and lives (dwells) within us; as Christians he helps and guides us in our daily lives. *Note: mention that anyone can say 'yes' to Jesus and have the Holy Spirit inside them, and that after the service, you are happy to pray with them if that is what they would like.*

▶ 8.42 pm   Video song   4 min

'Welcome Holy Spirit': **youtu.be/c8M1SvGuSjo**

8.46 pm   Final prayer and finish   2 min

8.48 pm   End

WHAT ABOUT POLITICS, PEACE, REFUGEES, HOPE AND WAR? (FIVE SESSIONS)

This series of five sessions looks at some of the big questions in society. Session 5, 'What about war?', was delivered near Remembrance Day, so unless you are delivering this at the same time of year, you will probably need to amend the session substantially. Or you could simply miss it out.

1 What about politics?

1 TIMOTHY 2:1–2; MATTHEW 22:17–21

Resources: name labels; ice-breaker PowerPoint questions; prayer labels and pens; drinks and cakes/doughnuts; video countdown timer; game resources; 'House of Commons' video clip; badges/placards for sausage and hot dog debate, pens, voting slips and ballot box; *Amazing Grace* trailer video; 'Amazing Grace (My Chains Are Gone)' video song

🚩 7 00 pm   Doors open   30 min

Name labels given out, prayer labels and pens distributed around tables, drinks and cakes/doughnuts served, ice-breaker questions on screen.

▶ 7.25 pm   Video countdown timer   5 min

🚩 7.30 pm   Game   10 min

💬 7.40 pm   Notices and encouragements   5 min

▶ 7.45 pm   Video clip   5 min

This clip features moments of John Bercow as Speaker of the House of Commons: **youtu.be/O-djMYYIvyE**

💬 7.50 pm   Link   3 min

See if people can guess this evening's theme.

🚩 7.53 pm   Table group activity   7 min

What is politics? Discuss in table groups and then feed back answers.

8.00 pm   Whole group activity   10 min

Light-hearted debate between two people about whether to have sausages or hot dogs next week. (Two team members should be briefed in advance, one representing the 'Sausage Party' and the other the 'Hot Dog Party'. Then people get an opportunity to vote. The most popular food will then be served next week. Create billboards for each party member to hold up.

8.10 pm   Table group activity   15 min

Should politics and the church mix? In other words, should the church (or Christians) get involved with politics? Ask people to discuss the question in their table groups and then feed back their answers.

8.25 pm   Video clip   4 min

Trailer for the movie *Amazing Grace*, the story of William Wilberforce: **youtu.be/Q6Cv5P9H9qU**

8.29 pm   Talk   5 min

Within the talk reflect on the film drawing out how, as a Christian, William Wilberforce fought for the rights of slaves. Think about where we may want to see change for people who are deprived.

8.34 pm   Video song   5 min

'Amazing Grace (My Chains Are Gone)' by Chris Tomlin: **youtu.be/QBRwoqJP2sk**

8.39 pm   Final prayer and finish   2 min

8.41 pm   End

The great sausage or hot dog debate voting slip

Please enter an X into one of the two choices below.

Leaving this ballot paper blank or entering an X in both choices will invalidate your voting slip.

☐   Sausages

☐   Hot dogs

2 What about peace?

PHILIPPIANS 4:7

Resources: name labels; ice-breaker PowerPoint questions; prayer labels and pens; drinks and prepared meal (food that won the vote last week); video countdown timer; game resources; *shalom* word search; images of peace (candle, sleeping baby, waterfall, etc.); meditation script, candle.

7.00 pm   Doors open   30 min

Name labels given out, prayer labels and pens distributed around tables, drinks served, ice-breaker questions on screen.

7.30 pm   Meal (food that won the vote last week)   30 min

7.55 pm   Video countdown timer   5 min

8.00 pm   Game   10 min

8.10 pm   Notices and encouragements   5 min

8.15 pm   Table group activity   6 min

A word search based on the different meanings of *shalom* – use an online word search generator to produce this. Suggested words: complete; contentment; fullness; harmony; health; peace; prosperity; rest; safety; security; tranquillity; welfare; wellness; wholeness

8.21 pm   Intro link   3 min

Ask if people can guess the theme, based on what they have read in the word search? Then explain that we are looking at the meaning of *shalom*, which although some of us know this word as the Hebrew word for peace, means so much more than just peace.

8.24 pm   Table discussion 8 min

Invite people to look again at the words from the word search. Discuss what they mean. Which ones are important to us? Any we don't understand?

8.32 pm   Whole group activity   7 min

Prior to the service starting, you need to have put up around the room different peaceful images. For the activity, people are asked to move around the church and choose three images which help them to either feel peaceful or help them to identify with some of the words in the word search. Get people to feed back their thoughts, etc.

8.39 pm   Whole group activity   5 min

A simple, spoken meditation, either ad-libbed or written beforehand, helping people to discover five minutes of peace, rest, contentment, etc. See the example below. Light a candle, dim the lights and invite people to relax.

8.44 pm   Final prayer and finish   2 min

Explain that there is no rush to leave straight away, if people want to continue sitting in peace. Also, people may have become aware how much peace they are lacking in their lives, and so we are happy to pray with them, etc.

8.46 pm   End

A meditation

If possible, dim the lights and stand a lit candle on a small table. Explain that we are going to pray in a bit of a different way, by using our imagination. We are going to imagine meeting Jesus. Encourage people to be quiet and get themselves in a comfortable position. Speak calmly and gently. Don't rush what you are saying.

Close your eyes and relax... As you inhale, breathe in the peace of God... As you breathe out, breath out any distractions in your mind... Breath in the peace of God... Breath out any worries or fear... Breath in the peace of God... Breath out anger... Keep breathing in and out. Concentrate on relaxing, right from the tip of your toes to the top of your head... Keep deep breathing in and out.

Now, imagine that it's a lovely summer's day. You're sat on the bank of a little, gently flowing stream and you're dangling your feet in the water. You can feel the soft, green grass under your hands... Keep deeply breathing in and out...

In the distance, you see someone coming towards you, walking along the bank of the stream. As they get closer, you can see that it's Jesus. What does he look like? As he comes closer, you stand up and run over to him. Jesus smiles and gives you the biggest hug, lifting you off your feet... Keep deeply breathing in and out... You feel very safe... and very loved...

What do you tell Jesus? What do you share with him? How does he respond? Keep deeply breathing in and out...

Jesus listens to you, while tenderly reminding you that you are loved... and valued... and forgiven...

As you talk to Jesus, the weight of all your worries and fears seems to fade away. You feel so free and light, like you could almost float away...

Jesus gently stands you back on your feet and gives you one last hug... Keep breathing deeply breathing in and out...

As you watch Jesus walk back along the bank of the stream, you feel relaxed and content. You sit back down, dangle your feet in the water once again... Keep deeply breathing in and out... Breath in the peace of Jesus... Breath out fear... and when you're ready, open your eyes...

3 What about refugees?

MATTHEW 25:35–40

Resources: name labels; ice-breaker PowerPoint questions; prayer labels and pens; drinks and cakes/doughnuts; video countdown timer; game resources; first refugee video clip; list of items for interactive table activity; 'Journey' story for whole group activity, lining paper for movement board; second refugee video clip; written reflection

🚩 **7.00 pm   Doors open   30 min**

Name labels given out, prayer labels and pens distributed around tables, drinks and cakes/doughnuts served, ice-breaker questions on screen.

▶ **7.25 pm   Video countdown timer   5 min**

🚩 **7.30 pm   Game   10 min**

🎬 **7.40 pm   Notices and encouragements   5 min**

▶ **7.45 pm   Intro and video clip   6 min**

Introduce the theme of refugees and then show the video clip about the plight of refugees: **youtu.be/pxUpIjVdpRo**

⚑ 7.51 pm   Table group activity   8 min

Table groups are given a list of 15 different things that they might want to take with them, if they suddenly had to leave their homes and become refugees. Each table group choose six things from their list that they would take with them. Get feedback afterwards.

Print these out, ideally with pictures: food, water, pets, spare clothes, photo album, passport, computer, money, weapons, mobile phone, spare shoes, medicine, old or sick family members, a cooking pot and a map.

🔲 7.59 pm   Link talk   2 min

Link the previous activity with next activity, explaining that having thought about what it's like to 'suddenly leave their homes', we are now going to imagine the hardships and challenges that refugees have to face, when they are trying to get to a country of safety.

⚑ 8.01 pm   Whole group activity   10 min

You will need a long roll of paper (like lining paper). Divide the paper into 23 sections or squares. Each section needs to be approximately 12" deep. Number each section 1 to 23. The whole congregation is invited to come to the back of church, as they are going to begin their 'journey' as refugees. An Ignite team member reads out the stages of a refugee's journey and depending on which items each table group has chosen in the earlier activity, each group will gradually move the right number of squares of the 'board' forwards or backwards. At the end of the journey story, there may or may not be a table group that has successfully 'won' by arriving at a place of safety. Afterwards, get feedback on how different groups felt, etc.

▶ 8.11 pm   Video clip   7 min

This film has lots of different refugees who have ended up in a place of safety talking about their experiences as refugees and about what their lives are like now: **youtu.be/8bEK6gytwec**

8.18 pm   Reflection   4 min

An ad-lib reflection on what it is like to be a refugee and their experiences, and how we view and treat refugees, using the words 'I wonder' to begin many of the reflection's sentences.

8.22 pm   Final prayer and finish   2 min

8.24 pm   End

Refugee journey game

- As a family group you all leave your home country, the only place you have ever known because you believe that if you stay you will all die. You are fearful but relieved to have finally made the decision – **move forward 5 spaces**.

- You begin to walk, it's an exhausting journey. If you have an elderly relative with you **go back 2 spaces**.

- The weather is hot, you need water. If you have water **move forward 2 spaces**.

- You are walking all day every day; your feet are hot, swollen and painful! If you packed spare shoes in your luggage, you can change your shoes and help relieve the pressure on your feet so you can walk a bit quicker – **move forward 2 spaces**. If you don't have spare shoes, you will need to walk barefoot – **go back 1 space**.

- You are hungry, some of you have food with you but it has been heavy to carry and is slowing you down! Others have begged for food on the journey or found food on trees, bushes and fields. You eat and feel more energised – **move forward 2 spaces**.

- You arrive at the sea and need to pay for a place on a boat. If you have money, you board the boat – **move forward 3 spaces**. If you don't have money, you need to stay and find work.

- Food is hard to find. If you have a domestic animal with you, are you prepared to kill it? *(Pause to find out answer.)* If you have that card and as a group are prepared to kill it, **move forward 5 spaces**.

- Malaria strikes your family; this is an easily treated condition with the right medication. If you have medication **move forward 1 space**. If you don't have medicine, sadly the youngest member of your family is not strong enough to fight the disease and dies – **the youngest member of the 'family' sits down**.

- The two leading groups get sent to a refugee camp, where it has been agreed that you are refugees in need of safety in a safe country. If you have a passport, it has been easy to check your ID – **move forward 2 spaces**.

- If you have weapons on you, these are unhelpful to you as you are perceived to be dangerous to other people. You are arrested and detained.

- That's where we will end this journey. How has the journey been for you?

4 What about hope?

1 PETER 3:15

Resources: name labels; ice-breaker PowerPoint questions; prayer labels and pens; drinks and prepared meal; video countdown timer; game resources; video clip about hope; 'What sort of things do we hope for?' PowerPoint; two long pieces of paper, marker pens; prepared talk; background video song

7.00 pm   Doors open   30 min

Name labels given out, prayer labels and pens distributed around tables, drinks served, ice-breaker questions on screen.

7.30 pm   Meal   30 min

7.55 pm   Video countdown timer   5 min

8.00 pm   Game   10 min

8.10 pm   Notices and encouragements   5 min

8.15 pm   Video clip   4 min

This is a video clip about hope: **youtu.be/dvw4zguM__w**

8.19 pm   Table group discussion   6 min

Question – what sort of things do we hope for? (Put this question up on PowerPoint.) Then get feedback.

🚩 **8.25 pm**   Whole group activity   12 min

You will need two long pieces of paper. On the first piece of paper, invite people to come up and write down words that describe what they feel when they feel hopeless. On the second piece of paper, invite people to write down words that describe what they feel when they feel hopeful. Then get feedback.

💬 **8.37 pm**   Talk   5 min

See the suggested talk below or write your own on the idea of Christian hope and what it means to put our hope in God.

🚩 **8.42 pm**   Response (video song in the background)   5 min

Invite people to come forward for prayer if they would like to receive Jesus into their lives, so they can also have an 'everlasting hope':
youtu.be/9KIhYZQ_ovw

💬 **8.47 pm**   End

Points you may want to include in the talk

- Christian hope is different from non-Christian hope.
- Non-Christian hope is a bit like making a wish: 'I hope I get a job'; 'I hope I don't get cancer'; 'I hope my kid gets the school of their choice.'
- Christian hope is based on certainty – it's a secure hope based on the reality of Jesus – who he is and what he has done for us, e.g. John 3:16.
- It's also based on a Christian understanding of what is going to happen in the future – John 14.
- Because we have such a certain hope, we can be more secure and feel safe regardless of what life may throw at us. You could liken this to when the disciples thought they were going to drown and Jesus calmed the storm – Mark 4:35–41.
- Anyone can exchange their 'wish list' hope for a certain hope by saying sorry for the stuff they've done wrong and inviting Jesus into their lives – Romans 10:9.

5 What about war?

ECCLESIASTES 3:8

Resources: name labels; ice-breaker PowerPoint questions; prayer labels and pens; drinks and jam sandwiches; video countdown timer; game resources; World War I quiz, paper and pens; poppy-making materials; final episode from *Blackadder Goes Forth*; large wooden cross, blue tack; 'In Flanders Fields' poem

7.00 pm   Doors open   30 min

Name labels given out, prayer labels and pens distributed around tables, drinks served, ice-breaker questions on screen. During this time, serve jam sandwiches as a nod to what soldiers in the trenches would have eaten during World War I.

7.25 pm   Video countdown timer   5 min

7.30 pm   Notices and encouragements   10 min

7.40 pm   Intro and whole group activity   10 min

Introduce the theme and create a suitable quiz for your guests.

7.50 pm   Craft activity   10 min

Make paper poppies. *Note: source a method for doing this from YouTube.*

▶ **8.00 pm   Video   30 min**

Watch *Blackadder Goes Forth*, season 4, episode 6, 'Goodbyeee'. *Note: you will need to buy this. Also make sure you have the appropriate licence, as you are showing a whole programme.*

🚩 **8.30 pm   Whole group activity   8 min**

This is designed to be a simple act of Remembrance. While someone reads the poem 'In Flanders Fields' by John McCrae, people are invited to bring up the poppies that they made earlier and stick them on a large wooden cross. This is followed by a very short time of simple prayer.

8.38 pm   Final prayer and finish   2 min

8.41 pm   End

EASTER (THREE SESSIONS)

This series is designed to introduce people to the themes of Palm Sunday, the last supper, and Jesus' eventual crucifixion and resurrection.

It also gives them the opportunity of sharing in bread and wine without calling it 'Communion' (which is helpful if you don't have a clergy person available).

The third session is quite extensive, so it will need a little thinking through to ensure that you know exactly what you are doing. We usually do an Easter series so that we end with crucifixion the week before Holy week. We then tend to break for two weeks and return with a look at resurrection and enjoy a celebratory party together. In this Easter series we combined both the crucifixion and the resurrection in session 3. If it suits you better, you may wish to do this over a two-week period before and after Easter.

1 Palm Sunday

MATTHEW 21:1–11

Resources: ice-breaker PowerPoint questions; name labels and pens; prayer cards; video countdown timer; drinks and prepared meal; game resources; kingly attributes sheets, pens and paper; a prepared 'Jesus' kingly attributes' word search; S.M. Lockridge video clip.

7.00 pm   Doors open   30 min

Name labels given out, prayer labels and pens distributed around tables, drinks served, ice-breaker questions on screen.

7.25 pm   Video countdown timer   5 min

7.30 pm   Meal   30 min

8.00 pm   Game   10 min

8.10 pm   Notices and encouragements   5 min

8.15 pm   Whole group activity   8 min

What things and attributes does a king have? Get people to move around and look at different attributes put up around the room and ask them to choose the five things they think a king is most likely to have. Then get feedback.

8.23 pm   Link talk   2 min

Jesus was welcomed into Jerusalem like a king, but he didn't have any of the things and attributes that we normally associate with a king.

8.25 pm   Table group activity   8 min

Hand out word searches to each person. Get them to do the word search, and then discuss briefly among themselves which of Jesus' kingly attributes most surprised them or interested them. Were there any other attributes that they think Jesus has that weren't included in the word search? Then get feedback.

8.33 pm   Link talk   2 min

Underline the fact that these words are not enough to describe Jesus and do him justice! Jesus – the humble servant king who rode into Jerusalem on a donkey – is so much more than that. And here is one man's (Dr S.M. Lockridge) attempt to describe him more fully...

8.35 pm   Video clip   4 min

Dr S.M. Lockridge's description of Jesus: **youtu.be/yzqTFNfeDnE**

8.39 pm   Closing prayer and finish 2 min

Mention anything being given away, and that prayer and chat is available, etc. as people leave.

8.41 pm   End

List of kingly possessions and attributes to post around the church

Wealthy
Palace
Army
Government
Crown Jewels
Warrior
Strong
Privileged
Coat of arms
Ruthless
Nice clothes
Well educated
Servants
Royal carriage

Word search terms

There are many free, printable word search generators available online.

DEFENDER
FAIR
FORGIVING
HONEST
HUMBLE
KIND
LIBERATING
LOVING
MERCIFUL
PERFECT
POWERFUL
SAVIOUR
SERVANT
VICTORIOUS
WISE

2 The last supper

MARK 14:12–31

Resources: ice-breaker PowerPoint questions; name labels and pens; drinks and cakes/doughnuts; video countdown timer; games resources; video clip from *Shrek 2*; assorted choices of tableware; question sheet for 'Last meal' discussion; video clip from *Miracle Maker*; prepared talk; bread and non-alcoholic wine; Matt Redman's 'Remembrance' video song

7.00 pm   Doors open   30 min

Name labels given out, prayer labels and pens distributed around tables, drinks and cakes/doughnuts served, ice-breaker questions on screen.

7.25 pm   Video countdown timer   5 min

7.30 pm   Game   10 min

7.40 pm   Notices and encouragements   5 min

7.45 pm   Video clip   3 min

Video clip from *Shrek 2* – the 'dinner with the parents' scene:
youtu.be/ODOchrd6-P8

7.48 pm   Table group discussion – memorable meal   6 min

What is the most memorable/weird/funny/best/worst meal that people have ever had? Then get feedback.

7.54 pm   Whole group activity   10 min

Setting the table: each table group is invited in turn to pick something from an assorted range of tableware and place it on a table which is needing to be made ready for a meal. Keep doing this until people think the table is ready.

8.04 pm   Table group discussion   6 min

Last meal: linking to the previous activity, give each table group a sheet with these three questions on it: *If you were having one last important meal at the table we've just prepared before going away for a long time: 1 – Who would you invite? 2 – What would you say? 3 – What would you do?* Then get feedback.

8.10 pm   Link talk   2 min

Briefly explain the context of the last supper, that is, how and why Jesus and the disciples have arrived at this point. Don't upstage the coming talk!

8.12 pm   Video clip   6 min

Video clip about the last supper, from *The Miracle Maker*: **youtu.be/EIrN9RJhbi0**

8.18 pm   Talk   5 min

Use the themes of the evening to focus on the fact that Jesus is real and relational, that he used everyday things and events to help people remember important things, and that he is the humble servant king who came to sacrifice himself to save us.

8.23 pm   Whole group activity   6 min

Bread and wine: while showing the video song 'Remembrance' by Matt Redman, invite people to come up to the table and take a piece of bread dipped into some wine, as they remember the reality of who Jesus is and what he has done for them: **youtu.be/9oCNwIA6xLc**

8.29 pm   Finish   2 min

As people leave, mention that people are available if they need to chat or want to pray with somebody.

8.31 pm   End

3 Arrest, crucifixion and resurrection

LUKE 22:47—24:12

Resources: ice-breaker PowerPoint questions; name labels and pens; drinks and cakes/doughnuts; video countdown timer; game resources; Easter quiz questions and answers; cut-up Holy Week timeline events (one set per table), A4 paper and glue sticks; enacted Bible reading; crossbeam, nails and wine vinegar; resurrection video clip; Rend Collective 'Resurrection Day' video song

7.00 pm   Doors open   30 min

Name labels given out, prayer labels and pens distributed around tables, drinks and cakes/doughnuts served, ice-breaker questions on screen

7.25 pm   Video countdown timer   5 min

7.30 pm   Game   10 min

7.40 pm   Notices and encouragements   5 min

7.45 pm   Whole group activity   7 min

Light-hearted quiz about Easter. *Note: you will need to create this quiz.*

7.52 pm   Table group activity   6 min

Hand out cut-up timeline events to table groups and ask them to see if they can put the different events of Holy Week in the right order. Then get feedback.

7.58 pm   Interactive link activity – timeline 5 min

See what people remember about Palm Sunday and the last supper, from the previous two sessions. Then move them on to the Garden of Gethsemane via the link intro.

8.03 pm   Link intro to Jesus in the garden   2 min

Briefly set the scene, then go into the enacted Bible reading.

8.05 pm   Enacted Bible reading – Mark 14   7 min

After the Bible reading (see below), ask people what they think Jesus felt about his friends not being able to stay awake while he prayed.

8.12 pm   Link intro to Good Friday 2 min

Talk about the horror of the humiliation, beating and crucifixion that Jesus suffered.

8.14 pm   Interactive moving around activities   10 min

1 *Cross-beam:* Invite people to feel what it was like on the cross, by holding the beam across their shoulders.
2 *Nails:* Invite people to take some nails and imagine what it would have been like to have them pierce their own hands and feet. Perhaps have enough nails so people can take a couple home.
3 *Red wine vinegar:* Get people to taste the bitter sourness of some red wine vinegar, which is what Jesus was offered while on the cross.

8.24 pm   Link to Jesus' resurrection   2 min

Explain where we are up to, that is, Jesus has died and has been buried and everyone thought that was the end of the story!

▶ 8.26 pm   Video clip   5 min

Jesus' resurrection. After the video, briefly explain why this is good news!
youtu.be/HaS-9AP96gE

8.31 pm   Finish and play video song as people leave 2 min

As people leave remind them that prayer is available. Play 'Resurrection
Day' by Rend Collective: **youtu.be/9u7V-g_cJaU**

8.33 pm   End

Sentences for Easter timeline

Jesus' entry into Jerusalem on a donkey.
Jesus clears the temple.
Jesus shares the last supper with his disciples.
Jesus sweats blood in the Garden of Gethsemane, while the disciples sleep.
Jesus is arrested.
Jesus appears before the Sanhedrin (Jewish court).
Jesus appears before Pontius Pilate and is sentenced to be crucified.
Jesus is crucified with two criminals and dies.
Jesus is buried in a tomb.
Jesus is resurrected three days later.

Enacted Bible reading

Mark 14:32–46 (adapted from NLT)

Narrator: They went to the olive grove called Gethsemane, and Jesus said…

Jesus: 'Sit here while I go and pray.'

Narrator: He took Peter, James and John with him, and he became deeply troubled and distressed. He told them…

Jesus: 'My soul is crushed with grief to the point of death. Stay here and keep watch with me.'

Narrator: He went on a little farther and fell to the ground. He prayed that, if it were possible, the awful hour awaiting him might pass him by. He cried out…

Jesus: 'Abba, Father, everything is possible for you. Please take this cup of suffering away from me. Yet I want your will to be done, not mine.'

Narrator: Then he returned and found the disciples asleep. He said to Peter…

Jesus: 'Simon, are you asleep? Couldn't you watch with me even one hour? Keep watch and pray, so that you will not give in to temptation. For the spirit is willing, but the body is weak.'

Narrator: Then Jesus left them again and prayed the same prayer as before. When he returned to them again, he found them sleeping, for they couldn't keep their eyes open. And they didn't know what to say. When he returned to them the third time, he said…

Jesus: 'Go ahead and sleep. Have your rest. But no – the time has come. The Son of Man is betrayed into the hands of sinners. Up, let's be going. Look, my betrayer is here!'

Narrator: And immediately, even as Jesus said this, Judas, one of the twelve disciples, arrived with a crowd of men armed with swords and clubs. They had been sent by the leading priests, the teachers of religious law and the elders. The traitor, Judas, had given them a prearranged signal: 'You will know which one to arrest when I greet him with a kiss. Then you can take him away under guard.' As soon as they arrived, Judas walked up to Jesus. 'Rabbi!' he exclaimed, and gave him the kiss. Then the others grabbed Jesus and arrested him.

CHRISTMAS (THREE SESSIONS)

This series will take a little pre-planning…

First, you will have to create your own big, homemade Ignite Advent calendar. We made one on a large noticeboard with just four windows to open. Each of the first three windows to be opened revealed that week's theme. The fourth window was opened at our Christmas party and showed the nativity scene.

Second, you will need to find a simple craft activity for each week's theme, which you should be able to find online.

Have fun!

1 The role of the angels

LUKE 1:26–38; MATTHEW 1:18–20; LUKE 2:9–15

'Angels from the realms of glory'

Resources: name labels; drinks and cakes/doughnuts; pens; ice-breaker PowerPoint questions; prayer cards; video countdown timer; game resources; large homemade Advent calendar, chocolates; angel and Mary video clip; three angel stories from the gospels (several copies on separate sheets); angel craft-making materials; 'Angels from the realms of glory' or 'Hark the herald angels sing' video hymn

🚩 7.00 pm   Doors open   30 min

Name labels given out, prayer labels and pens distributed around tables, drinks and cakes/doughnuts served, ice-breaker questions on screen.

▶ 7.25 pm   Video countdown timer   5 min

🚩 7.30 pm   Game   10 min

Christmas movie quiz. *Note: for this Christmas series, we used a quiz from YouTube with 100 questions:* **youtu.be/Kg2ulnD-XXo** (Each question will need to be paused just before the answer comes up.)

📹 7.40 pm   Notices and encouragements   5 min

▐ **7.45 pm**   Advent calendar 5 min

Open the Ignite Advent calendar, explain the theme (angels) and hand out chocolates. *Note: your Advent calendar should be large and homemade, with each week's theme depicted with a picture, etc.*

▐ **7.50 pm**   Whole group activity   6 min

Mark out a long '0–100' scale on the floor, and invite people to stand somewhere along the scale to show how much they believe in angels, with 0 being 'Don't believe at all' and 100 being 'Completely believe'. Then take feedback from people.

▶ **7.56 pm**   Video clip   4 min

The angel speaking to Mary: **youtu.be/Z1OLLwtCqtM**

▭ **8.00 pm**   Link   3 min

Say something like: *'While some of us may find it difficult to believe in angels, there are lots of instances in the Bible where angels have appeared and spoken to many different people. So, as far as Christians are concerned, they are very much real!'*

▐ **8.03 pm**   Table group discussion   8 min

Hand out one of three New Testament angel stories to each table group. Ask them to discuss the following question: what is the role/job of the angel? What makes this story important? Then get feedback. The passages we used were Luke 1:26–38; Matthew 1:18–20; Luke 2:9–15.

▭ **8.11 pm**   Sum-up feedback   3 min

▐ **8.14 pm**   Individual craft activity   10 min

Make an angel. *Note: there are various examples of angel-making crafts on the internet. Please find one that suits your congregation.*

8.24 pm   Whole group activity   4 min

Explain that as we have been thinking about angels, and so as we are also getting into the festive spirit, we thought that we should finish this evening by singing the first verse and chorus of 'Angels from the realms of glory' or 'Hark the herald angels sing'. It will be good practice for all the other carols that they will be singing in the coming few weeks!

8.28 pm   Sum-up, final prayer and finish   2 min

8.30 pm   End

2 The role of the wise men

MATTHEW 2:1–12

'We three kings'

Resources: ice-breaker questions PowerPoint; name labels, pens; prayer cards; drinks and prepared meal; video countdown timer; game resources; homemade Advent calendar and chocolates; sketch scripts for three people, props, 'Yakety Sax' music; prepared talk; small gift box template, pens, glue sticks or Sellotape; 'We three kings' video song

🏳 **7.00 pm Doors open 30 min**

Name labels given out, prayer labels and pens distributed around tables, drinks served, ice-breaker questions on screen.

🏳 **7.30 pm Meal 30 min**

▶ **7.55 pm Video countdown timer 5 min**

🏳 **8.00 pm Game 10 min**

Christmas movie quiz. *Note: for this Christmas series, we used a quiz from YouTube with 100 questions:* **youtu.be/Kg2ulnD-XXo**

💬 **8.10 pm Notices and encouragements 5 min**

🏳 **8.15 pm Advent calendar 5 min**

Open the Ignite Advent calendar, explain the theme (the wise men) and hand out chocolates. *Note: your Advent calendar should be large and homemade, with each week's theme depicted with a picture, etc.*

▶   8.20 pm   Sketch   5 min

This sketch (see below) is about the three wise men/kings shopping for presents for Jesus. *Note: you will need the 'Yakety Sax' music from the Benny Hill comedy programmes, for when the kings are rushing around:* **youtu.be/3WShMzwT-nM**

🚩   8.25 pm   Table group activity   6 min

Ask the question: why did the wise men/kings go and see Jesus? Then get feedback.

💬   8.31 pm   Talk   5 min

This would be done best as an ad-lib talk, based on the feedback from the previous table discussion.

🚩   8.36 pm   Whole group activity   10 min

Gift box craft activity: before guests stick the box together, invite them to write on the inside of the box what kind of personal 'gift' they would like to offer Jesus. Put up a PowerPoint screen with possible suggestions. Guests can choose to either take their box home or leave it to decorate the church. *Note: various gift box craft activities are available on the internet. Find one that is most suitable for your congregation.*

🚩   8.46 pm   Whole group activity   4 min

Sing along to the carol 'We three kings', pause after the first verse to say goodbye, etc. and then finish the carol if time allows: **youtu.be/zNBbCkDMSLw**

💬   8.50 pm   End

The three kings sketch

The three kings/wise men, are standing on stage, getting ready to go shopping.

King 1   Okay, guys, so we each know what we're buying, right? *(Other two kings agree enthusiastically.)* Stan, you're buying…

King 2   Frankincense!

King 1   Very good. And Jim, you're getting…

King 3   Myrrh…

King 1   Excellent! Awesome! And I'll buy the gold. Right then, let's hit those shops, get those bargains and then meet back here in an hour.

All three kings dash off in different directions, for a few moments, while some frantic music is playing in the background. When they come back, each is carrying a shopping bag.

King 2   Phew! That was hard work.

King 3   Tell me about it! The shops were heaving. I've lost count of how many times my toes have been trodden on.

King 1   Never mind all that! Did you get the gifts?

King 2   Yeah, got the frankincense. Mind you, the shopkeeper also tried to sell me a thurible – whatever that is.

King 1   No idea, mate. Still, well done on getting the frankincense. And Jim, did you get the myrrh?

King 3   Oh yes, Fred, it's in the bag! Get it – in the bag?

King 1   Shut up, you twit! Alright then *(ticks off gifts on his fingers)*, frankincense, myrrh and I managed to get the gold. So, we're sorted. Three awesome gifts, for an awesome Saviour! Well done, lads. *(Other two kings look pleased, perhaps high-fiving each other.)* Right then, we've got a star to follow, so we'd better be off!

The three kings leave the stage. Someone briefly comes on stage carrying a large sign that says, 'Many months later, on the way back from Bethlehem...' The three kings trudge on to the stage, one after the other, with King 3 following last.

King 3	Would it make any difference if I said I'm sorry?

King 1   Oooh, I don't know... Why don't you say it and see what happens?

King 3   I'm really, very, very sorry...

King 1   Shaddup!

King 2   You got to admit, it was just a little bit funny.

King 1   Funny! Funny, he says! Here we are at the most amazing event in the whole of history, and you think that was a bit funny?

King 3   Honestly, I'm really sorr–

King 1   Shaddup! It was a beautiful moment... There he was, the baby Jesus, looking all beautiful and special, lying asleep in the manger, his mum Mary sat next him and Joseph standing proud and tall. We bow down, cos after all, he is the Messiah, the Saviour of the world. And then we get out the gifts. I get out the gold – pure, expensive, fit for a king. Stan, you give Jesus the frankincense, cos he's worthy of our worship. And then, Jim, just remind me again, what gift did you give King Jesus?

King 3   (*Mumbles incoherently.*)

King 1   Speak up! The nice ladies and gentlemen can't hear you. What did you give Jesus, after we gave him gold and frankincense?

King 3   (*Speaking very apologetically.*) An Olly Murs CD.

King 1   Yes, that's right. You gave the Saviour of the world – the Saviour of the world – an Olly Murs CD! You twit! You were meant to buy myrrh, what you anoint with, not Murs that you listen to. I tell you what, I have never been so embarrassed in all my life!

King 3   I am so sorr –

King 1   Shaddup!

King 2   Still, look on the bright side…

King 1   And what's that, then?

King 2   At least we've got something to listen to on the way back home!
            (Freeze and cue Olly Murs song.)

3 The role of the shepherds

LUKE 2:8–20

'While shepherds watched their flocks'

Resources: name labels; drinks, mince pies and Christmas treats; pens; ice-breaker PowerPoint questions; prayer cards; video countdown timer; Christmas movie quiz; homemade Advent calendar and chocolates; game resources; Jewish shepherd video clip; shepherd sketch scripts x 2; notes for ad-lib talk; sheep-making craft activity resources; 'While shepherds watched' video song with lyrics

7.00 pm   Doors open   30 min

Name labels given out, prayer labels and pens distributed around tables, drinks and food served, ice-breaker questions on screen.

7.25 pm   Video countdown timer   5 min

7.30 pm   Game   10 min

Christmas movie quiz. *Note: for this Christmas series, we used a quiz from YouTube with 100 questions:* **youtu.be/Kg2ulnD-XXo**

7.40 pm   Notices and encouragements   5 min

Promote the Christmas party if you are having one next week.

7.45 pm   Advent calendar 5 min

Open the Ignite Advent calendar, explain the theme (shepherds) and hand out chocolates. *Note: your Advent calendar should be large and homemade, with each week's theme depicted with a picture, etc.*

▶ **7.50 pm   Video clip   1 min**

Short film about a modern-day Jewish shepherd (only use the first 39 seconds): **youtu.be/dsIzobZDl_8**

⚑ **7.51 pm   Table group activity   6 min**

Ask table groups to talk about what they know about the life of a shepherd, then feed back their answers.

▶ **7.57 pm   Sketch   5 min**

Sketch about two shepherds (see below).

⚑ **8.02 pm   Table group activity   6 min**

Ask the table groups to talk about why God sent the shepherds to see the baby Jesus, then feed back.

💬 **8.08 pm   Sum-up with ad-lib talk   5 min**

⚑ **8.13 pm   Whole group activity   10 min**

Making a model sheep. *Note: there are many different sheep crafts available online. Use one that is appropriate to your congregation.*

⚑ **8.23 pm   Whole group activity   3 min**

Sing 'While shepherds watched their flocks': **youtu.be/EdASbgux6ds**
Pray and finish.

💬 **8.26 pm   End**

The shepherds sketch

Characters: Old Ezra (granddad figure); two children; two shepherds – young Ezra and Zacharia; angel voice; heavenly host (3–4 voices, speaking through a mic off-stage)

Suggested directions: The children can be acted by children or, for some comic value, by adults. The angel voice should be done by someone speaking into a mic off stage, so the voice comes through the sound system. Old Ezra should be leaning back on a chair, with the children sat at his feet. Young Ezra and Zacharia are each sat on a blanket, wearing the obligatory dressing gowns, with tea towels on their heads. Old Ezra and children are situated stage left, in a freeze. Young Ezra and Zacharia are situated stage right, also in a freeze.

Child 1　　Tell us a story, Granddad Ezra.

Child 2　　Yes, tell us the one about when you and Uncle Zacharia heard about baby Jesus! We like that one!

Old Ezra　　But you've heard that story a thousand times already.

Both children　　Pleeease!

Old Ezra　　*(Laughing.)* Alright, alright. I'll tell you the baby Jesus story… again! *(Looks into the distance, remembering when he was a young shepherd.)* Me and your Uncle Zach were sat around a campfire in the fields one night, watching over the sheep. As usual, I was having to listen to your uncle's terrible sheep jokes…

Ezra and children freeze. Attention moves to Zacharia and young Ezra, stage left.

Zacharia　　Ezra, Ezra!

Young Ezra　　What now?

Zacharia　　What do you get if you cross an angry sheep and a moody cow? *(Pauses.)* An animal that's in a baaaad moooood! *(Laughs at his own joke.)*

Young Ezra That's terrible!

Zacharia That's nothing! Wait till you hear this one! How many sheep does it take to knit a sweater? *(Pauses.)*

Young Ezra I don't kno–

Zacharia *(Interrupts.)* Don't be silly — sheep can't knit! *(Laughs uproariously.)* Get it? Can't knit!

Young Ezra *(Grumpily.)* Wish I knew a certain shepherd brother who couldn't speak.

Zacharia *(Still chuckling.)* Don't be so grumpy! I know you like them really. Anyway, it's not as if you've got much else to do. Listen to sheep jokes, watch the actual sheep or, failing that, look at the stars. Which reminds me… *(looks up)* lot of them out tonight – stars, I mean.

Young Ezra Yeah, loads of them! Hey, do you remember how Dad used to tell us that every star was an angel looking down on us from heaven?

Zacharia Oh, yeah, he did, didn't he? In fact, what was it he used to say on nights like this? *(Speaks in an old man's voice.)* Eee, lad, all them stars mean that the…

Together … heavenly host is paying us a visit! *(Both laugh.)*

Zacharia Mind you, I never quite understood why he thought a heavenly host of angels would want to visit us? I mean, why would *anyone* want to visit a couple of boring, smelly shepherds, let alone a heavenly host? They'd only be interested in important people – not the likes of you and me! *(Notices that Ezra hasn't been properly listening to him and is looking intently down stage.)* Ezra? Ezra? What are you looking at?

Young Ezra The moon. It's very bright.

Zacharia *(Looking in the same direction as Ezra.)* Ezra, that can't be the moon!

Young Ezra Why not?

Zacharia   *(Points to stage left.)* Because the moon's over there!

Young Ezra *(Points down stage and speaking with a trembling voice.)* So what's that, then? Because whatever it is, it's getting brighter… *(Shields his eyes.)* Much brighter…

Both men fall to their knees, covering their eyes.

Angel voice Don't be afraid. I'm here to announce a great and joyful event that is meant for everybody, worldwide: a Saviour has just been born in King David's town, a Saviour who is the Messiah and Lord. This is what you're to look for: a baby wrapped in a blanket and lying in a manger.

Heavenly host   Alleluia! Glory to God in the highest! Peace on earth!

After a short pause, both men slowly stand up.

Young Ezra *(Speaking hesitantly.)* You… you know what… brother?

Zacharia   No, what?

Young Ezra I am never, ever, *ever* making fun of Dad again, because that… that… that was… was a real, honest to God…

Together   *(Both speaking excitedly.)* … heavenly host!

Both actors ad-lib, speaking over each other excitedly, saying things like 'Did you see that?', 'I don't believe it!', 'That angel!', 'So bright!', 'Baby?', 'Messiah?'

Young Ezra *(Starts rolling up his blanket.)* Right then, come on!

Zacharia   *(Starts gathering up his own blanket)* Where are we going?

Young Ezra Bethlehem, of course – King David's town. It's only a few miles away…

Zacharia   But what about the sheep?

Young Ezra We'll be back before sunrise. They won't even notice we're gone. Anyway, you said the heavenly host would never visit a couple of boring, smelly shepherds like us. Yet now it seems that we've been invited to meet the Saviour of the world! So come on, and don't tell him any of your sheep jokes when we get there – you'll make him cry!

Both actors freeze. Attention moves to Old Ezra and children, stage right.

Old Ezra And so that's what we did. Grabbed our blankets, left the sheep and ran all the way to Bethlehem! We weren't sure how we were going to find Jesus, but then Uncle Zach noticed this great big, bright star, hanging just above a stable. 'Ezra,' he said to me, 'that bright star looks a bit like the light we saw with the heavenly host.' So we went over. *(Looks at the children.)* And who did we find in a dirty old manger?

Both children *(Shout excitedly.)* Jesus!

Old Ezra That's right, Jesus. Mind you, we mustn't forget that his mum and dad were there as well, though they looked a bit surprised when us shepherds turned up to pay our respects. They probably thought we were coming to mug 'em! Still, once we told them about the angel and the heavenly host, they weren't so worried. In fact, Mary, Jesus' mum, smiled at us and asked us if we knew any jokes about sheep. I couldn't shut your Uncle Zack up for days afterwards!

Old Ezra and children freeze.

End

Tea break

Don't worry. Even though all the chocolate digestives are gone, we've brought some custard creams. We thought you deserved another break, since you've managed to stay with us.

So how are you doing? Has your brain been bamboozled with too much new information? Or is your mind swimming with your own thoughts, because God has been showing you what might be possible within your community?

Having got to the end of part III, maybe you've begun to dream about developing and launching your own Ignite service with the tools and ideas that we've shared with you. We hope so!

Frankly, though, even if you've decided that Ignite isn't the way to go, we really hope that you have been inspired to do *something* that engages with the people where you live. So, no hard feelings, and feel free to use whatever you've found to be useful to share Jesus with others.

On the other hand, if you're still with us, if you're still on track, then let's have a quick reminder of the stuff we've been thinking about since our last tea break.

Mind you, don't dunk your custard cream for too long as you're reading this!

First, we thought about food and the importance that it played both within Jesus' ministry as well as within the ministry of Ignite. We also explained that we are okay with people just coming and 'using us' to get fed, without staying for the rest of the service. Our aim is to give an unconditional and gracious welcome that allows the possibility of creating meaningful friendships.

Next, we considered that age-old Christian problem of how we measure success. We saw that baptisms, confirmations and even attendance figures don't necessarily give us an accurate picture of how we are doing. This led us to look at the 'theory of change', which was helpful, but still wasn't quite what we were looking for. In the end we adapted Michael Moynagh's and the Church Army's discipleship statements, which we found much easier to work with.

We then looked at our Ignite service checklist, our thoughts on everything you might possibly need to launch your own Ignite evening. We think it's a fairly comprehensive list, but please add to it if you think we've forgotten something (and let us know so we can add it to our own list). Just don't forget Kevin…

Finally, we gave you a load of Ignite service running orders – more than enough to keep you going for a few months. Which is pretty exciting!

And now, since you've just about finished your tea (although it does look like you managed to over-dunk a custard cream in there), let's move on to the last part of the book.

In some respects, part IV is the most important part of the book, since without it there would never have been a book in the first place. It tells the story of Ignite, right from its origins in a drug dealer's bedsit, being launched at St Paul's Church, Cliftonville, in 2007, through its expansion within Canterbury Diocese and the Channel Island of Guernsey to our most recent Ignite opening in Aylsham in 2023. Enjoy!

IV

THE STORY

16

How it all began

'For I was hungry and you gave me something to eat, I was thirsty and you gave me something to drink, I was a stranger and you invited me in, I needed clothes and you clothed me, I was ill and you looked after me, I was in prison and you came to visit me.' Then the righteous will answer him, 'Lord, when did we see you hungry and feed you, or thirsty and give you something to drink? When did we see you a stranger and invite you in, or needing clothes and clothe you? When did we see you ill or in prison and go to visit you?' The King will reply, 'Truly I tell you, whatever you did for one of the least of these brothers and sisters of mine, you did for me.'

MATTHEW 25:35–40 (NIV)

There is a contemporary Christian song called 'Beautiful Things' by Gungor that has pursued us now for a number of years, which we have used at Ignite and other contexts. It has uplifting, moving lyrics, which were complemented by a YouTube video that added even more depth to the song through clever storytelling. Be warned, though, you'll tear up! Anyway, we think that the lyrics beautifully captured what God was doing as he brought the Ignite project into being.

Check out the song and video at: **youtu.be/Is6weMrenls**

Ignite started in 2007 at St Paul's Church, Cliftonville, in Margate. The community of St Paul's at that time was the 18th poorest parish in the country. Cliftonville in Margate is a seaside town that had once been a sought-after holiday destination. Sadly, it began to go downhill when people moved their holidays from our seaside resorts and headed to Spain on the cheap package holidays of the 1970s.

In 2007 we had many people in our parish who were very poorly housed, accommodated in large ex-guest houses. These once beautiful buildings that were used to welcome people to their seaside holiday were now often owned by unscrupulous landlords and filled with individuals, couples or families needing cheap accommodation. Each rental consisted of just one room, with many sharing limited kitchen and bathroom facilities; they were known as houses of multiple occupation (HMOs). St Paul's Parish then had over 8,000 people within its boundary of one square mile without having a single tower block!

Many of the people living in these HMOs had complex needs. They were living on very low incomes, often had difficulties with addictions and were caught in the many social and economic problems that this way of living brings. Within the parish we also had a large amount of supported living houses. There was also a large Mencap residential centre, which also gave us people with learning difficulties to support in their spiritual needs too. St Paul's was a complex parish!

Ignite was our response to these various needs. So, sit back and let us let us tell you the story.

When we arrived in the parish in 2004, regular prayer walking around the parish was already well established. A team would meet and, according to the biblical principle of Mark 6:7, would go out in twos, asking God to put people in our path who he wanted us to engage with. And God did!

We'd spend time listening to people, because focusing on their needs and concerns was our priority. For example, if they needed food, we'd always offer to take them to a local café. We would sometimes be invited back to where they lived or we might just chat on a bench or in a café. If they needed clothing, we could signpost them into church, where we gave away donated clothes or suggest that they saw our own church welfare officer, who held a wealth of information to support people's needs.

The principle we worked under in this context was that – usually – we needed to look after people's physical needs before they were ready to receive any spiritual support. Why? Because their physical needs would have been deafening at the time. Then, if we felt prompted by God to do so, we would also chat to them about faith.

The faith bit of the conversation would always be gentle, making sure that what we said was also understandable. Nothing overwhelming, nothing heavy, not trying to get them to swallow a Bible. And then before leaving them, we would normally offer to pray for them. It didn't matter if they said no. After all, they have the right to choose! And anyway, we would still pray for them, once we moved on. The most important thing for us was that they'd had a positive encounter with two Christians. Working in this way gave us a great presence within the community and very often led to people coming into church.

We were quite tactical with the timing of our prayer walking. We would go out on a Monday afternoon, because on Tuesday mornings the church was open for free drinks and snacks, as well as prayer. This meant that people we spoke to while we were prayer walking could be offered the possibility to continue the conversation the next day in church. This was how we built relationships with our community, slowly being consistent, reliable and approachable.

A consequence of prayer walking was that a couple of our team built a relationship with a guy who happened to be a local drug dealer. He felt valued and cared for, and as a result was interested in what was being shared with him, and he invited them round to his tiny basement flat. Building on that invitation, while prayer walking the couple would often pop round to visit with chips for him and those he supplied drugs to. There they listened to people's needs without judgement, shared some biblical thoughts and offered prayer, all in simple, accessible words.

This eventually grew into a regular meeting and attracted more people, so that after a year or so the group became too big for the flat, and they asked if they could start meeting in the church. Unsurprisingly, we agreed. Suddenly we knew we had caught a tiger by the tail or we were riding a wave of the Spirit. Whatever it was, something amazing was happening! People who didn't come to church – who had probably never set foot in church, unless they were trying to nick the lead off the roof – were asking to come into our church, so they could talk to us about their lives and their questions about faith! This marked the moment when the church started being really accepted within that section of the community. It also showed us that they thought that Christianity – or at least this little local church – might have something positive to offer them.

It was these two groups – the chip-eating group and those we met prayer walking – that eventually led us to do an Alpha course for them in 2007. Just to confirm that we were still holding on to that tiger's tail, we also had what we believed was a miracle happen on that first night. We didn't know how many people would come along to this Alpha course, but we thought we would be very happy if 40 or 50 turned up. With that in mind, Debbie had baked 50 jacket potatoes. However, just before we opened the doors another team member arrived who had also cooked 50 jacket potatoes. Oops… So, now we had way too many potatoes. But when a hundred people walked through our doors, we thought, 'Yep, there's the tug of that tiger's tail again; we'd better hold on tight!'

We knew without doubt that God had intervened in the catering plans to make sure that everyone was fed. Thank goodness, as not having enough food was the last thing that this group of people needed! For the rest of the Alpha course, we had between 80 and 100 people turn up every week, and they were generously fed each and every single time.

Eventually, we finished the Alpha course, but amazingly, there were around 80 people who still wanted to carry on meeting. Bearing in mind that Alpha doesn't look much like Sunday church, and that most of them had never been to Sunday church, it didn't seem right to say to them, 'Right, then, that's Alpha finished with, so see you all on Sunday!' If we'd done that, their brains would have probably been scrambled, and we would have lost most of them within the first few weeks.

Instead, pretty much on the spur of the moment, we said, 'Come back next Wednesday.' From that point on, even though the look of Ignite has changed a little over the years, we have offered them food, friendship and an interactive fun way of engaging with faith. That was how Ignite was born in 2007. And to this day in 2024 the church still does Ignite every week at 7.00 pm on a Wednesday, which we are quite proud of.

If we're honest, we aren't people who work from vision statements or five-year plans or cleverly written church discipleship programmes. We are people who respond to what we see. In this case we saw a need for the people we were working with to do business with God in a different way to what was being offered on a Sunday. There wasn't anything wrong with Sunday church – it just seemed that something else was needed at this particular time and in this context.

The Bible tells us that God first loved us before we loved him, and that we should love our neighbour as ourselves. To us as individuals, this means that if God found it within himself to love us, then our natural response should be to intentionally love him back with all our heart, soul, strength and mind, and to share that love outwardly and intentionally with others, especially those who are hard to reach or marginalised by society.

Time and time again, scripture shows God lovingly reaching out even to those who don't care about him or those who other people would cross the street to avoid. How can we do any less? We knew that committing to this every week would be demanding, but they were more than worth it.

In 2013, we were approached by the Church Commissioners who were looking at new ways to build Christian communities. They wanted to look at what was working well and see if it could be replicated. They decided to come and visit our Wednesday evening Ignite but then arranged to come on a Thursday morning – which was a problem! We adapted to their needs, filmed Ignite and showed it to them the following morning in church, being careful to leave the previous night's crumbs on the floor to give them a true sense of Ignite!

This screening of Ignite resulted in us receiving a grant to employ two half-time mission enablers who were tasked with replicating Ignite in Ramsgate. Unfortunately, after two rounds of advertising, we were not able to fill the posts. After some consideration, Debbie and our Church Army colleague Stuart Budden, in conjunction with an enthusiastic parish team, replicated Ignite in Newington, Ramsgate in 2013, which ran until Covid lockdown in 2020.

The next stage of the Ignite story came in 2017, when the Church Commissioners essentially asked the diocese why they hadn't asked for funding to develop Ignite further. Following this we managed an expansion of Ignite communities with employed mission enablers replicating Ignite into areas of deprivation within the diocese of Canterbury.

These communities were started in Ashford, Maidstone, Sheerness, Herne Bay (two Ignites – one being a family's Ignite), Sittingbourne and Guernsey (at that time the Channel Islands fell under the care of Canterbury diocese). Sheerness sadly closed in 2023, when it was clear that the parish was unable to take over the responsibility of running Ignite when the enablers contracts ended.

Finally, the most recent Ignite started in Aylsham in November 2023. They are running a family's Ignite, like the one in Herne Bay. They have also found the Ignite material useful to use with their youth group.

Now in 2024, we are starting to look for new ideas. Debbie is exploring the possibility of Ignite working in a prison and within a rough sleeper centre. Who knows where the next stage of the journey will take us. We're just excited to see what God has planned for the future.

All said and done, it has been a rollicking, incredible ride, filled with laughter and tears, amazing God moments, hard times and wonderful times, and, dare we say, perfectly normal and boringly mundane stuff in between.

But God doesn't disappoint! Through conversation, a bad joke, a prayerful meditation, while munching on a hot dog or watching a film clip, God has shown up at every single Ignite session – in spades! Hallelujah!

Reflection

How willing am I to go out into my community without a personal plan?

How well do I know the needs of those in my community? Do they know me?

Am I too focused on church work within the building?

Prayer

Dear God, I so much want to make a difference in my community, but above all, I want to do what you are calling me to do within it. Help me to see things in a different way. Help me to see what you are doing within the community, and enable me to join in. In Jesus' name. Amen.

17

Some thoughts from our Ignite guests

Let the peace of Christ rule in your hearts, since as members of one body you were called to peace. And be thankful.
COLOSSIANS 3:15 (NIV)

Ignite really wouldn't be Ignite without the extended family of our Ignite guests. So we thought it would be good to share with you some direct quotes from people or some changes that we and others have witnessed in people's lives. These snapshots come from different Ignites within Canterbury Diocese and span across the years that Ignite has been running. We have altered names to protect people's identities.

* * *

Within this book we have tried to answer the difficult question of 'What is Ignite?' Hopefully we have gone some way to answering this question. We think that the best answer came from a guest in our first Ignite replication. His friend asked, 'What is Ignite?' He replied:

It's not like a church, it's not religious, more like a social club, but I have learnt a lot about God!

* * *

Over the years we have worked with many people with learning difficulties, welcoming them, accepting their differences and helping them – like others – to understand how faith is equally relevant to them. One such member said this about Ignite:

I come to Ignite because I like being around Christians and talk about the verses (Bible), and also, I like having a cup of tea here! Thank you!

On one occasion we were looking at the Trinity, not an easy concept for many people. We asked people to write down what they know about God, getting responses like: 'He made the world', 'He heals people', 'He forgives us', 'He doesn't exist'. We invited them to place what they had written on a big noticeboard, under a heading of Father, Son or Holy Spirit. Watching one member who has learning difficulties, with great excitement putting 'He baptised me' under Holy Spirit and re-affirming this to herself was amazing! Knowing that she was growing in her understanding and experience of faith was a privilege.

★ ★ ★

Ignite tries to meet people where they are and help them move forward in faith, while fully accepting and supporting them in the difficulties that they experience in life. One guest told us:

My faith has been challenged over the past couple of years and I've doubted, you know, God's deserted me, he's left me. And then I came here, and everyone sort of lifts me up. We have a chat and a prayer, and it puts everything back into perspective.

★ ★ ★

This work can be difficult. People come with different experiences and present challenges; they almost need to know that we will still care for them if they are difficult. Amanda came to Ignite following contact with the food bank; she was experiencing significant family difficulties and financial worries. We supported her with food and advice and provided her with pastoral support. Within an Ignite evening, she was difficult to manage – her need to get all she could for herself and her family led to her displaying a very selfish, lying attitude, which often disrupted the evenings. In truth she was quite a challenge to love.

From a very difficult beginning Ignite team members slowly built a relationship with her, and we saw a real change in her and the way she relates to others. She began to see a different way and started embracing new, healthier relationships and behaviours. We were seeing her display a kinder, more caring attitude towards others and their needs, replacing the 'angry at the world' attitude. We really saw her grow!

★ ★ ★

A couple who described themselves as having no friends came weekly and related well within the group. The man, who used to be a DJ and had very poor physical health, had his spirits lifted by being asked to help us with our sound system. He felt needed, while his wife enjoyed new-found friendships. They were open to what was being said to them about the Christian faith. We showed them love, saw their needs and created an environment within which they could come to faith.

* * *

Working with people who are battling addictions, we have seen them commit to faith and develop a will to change their lifestyle. Sadly, we have not seen instant freedom for people from addictions, but we have supported them through their journey to a life free from drugs.

Now, I come here, and I help, when (previously) I used to come here as an addict. I'm a strong person now; I pray a lot more.

Debbie had a soft spot for a local drug addict who, for many years, came into Ignite, mainly for food, begging for money or for a warm place to be. She was always rushing around needing money for her next fix. Debbie recalls: 'One evening she sat with me while Patrick led a meditation. As she relaxed, I could see her engaging with what was being said. When Patrick finished, she gave me a hug and said, "Debbie, there is a God, isn't there?"' Debbie agreed that she was right and that God loved her. She left Ignite happily, having made a connection with God, who knew her and loved her. Sadly, however, she died a few days later. Debbie knew that she had encountered God that night and felt God's tangible peace. She was engaging with God, and without Ignite this may never have happened for her.

* * *

Paul struggled with mental health issues and had been off work but felt safe and at home at Ignite. He accepted prayer and help regarding his challenges, and people noticed positive changes in his mood and confidence since accepting Jesus into his life.

* * *

Christine had her children taken into care and spent a short time in prison. She came to Ignite lonely and lost. It was here that she started enjoying life again:

It's nice that Christ is at the centre of it all. Games, loads of activities, quizzes and even craft activities!

* * *

For many people Ignite has become a place that they enjoy coming to. They meet with church friends and encounter God, who meets them where they are. Essentially all that Ignite is doing is creating an environment that promotes people engaging with God. We support the work that God is doing in their lives. It's not our work; it's God's!

I come into this place, and I go out feeling happier than when I come in. And I like to say a prayer… I light a candle… I wouldn't come here if I didn't like Ignite.

Conclusion

All the chocolate digestives and custard creams have gone, you've downed the last dregs of your tea (Is it just me – Patrick – that tries to lick out the biscuit bits from the inside of the cup? Debbie – Yes! Just you!) and we've arrived at the end of our time together.

If you are one of those folks who don't read a great deal, then thank you for sticking with it. On the other hand, if you normally read more theologically challenging and weightier stuff, then thank you also for even opening this book in the first place. Either way, we appreciate all of you, and we're genuinely grateful that you decided to spend some time finding out about Ignite.

While we don't see the need to look back on everything that we've covered, we hope that one thing has shone through all that you've read:

We believe – completely and utterly – that relationships are key!

Whether with your fellow church members, with your (soon to be, we hope) Ignite team or with everyday, ordinary people from your local community, relationships are absolutely key.

If you build genuine friendships with people, where you are willing to make yourself open and vulnerable, then you will earn the right to speak into people's lives and share your thoughts and ideas with them, especially when you want to share the good news of Jesus.

And if eventually you launch an Ignite, being so relationally minded will add to the quality of your welcome, because *everyone* will be treated as friends. It will also encourage people to participate and contribute, because we are obviously interested in what they think.

As we said in chapter 5, 'Belonging': 'There are no official or unofficial hoops to jump through or membership criteria to be met. People who come to Ignite automatically belong' (p. 32). Why? Because we are intentionally relational, and we want people to feel like they belong.

So, where to now? That's up to you.

Maybe it all sounds too much like hard work and it's just not for you, so you could consign this book to the shelf and forget about it. In which case, no hard feelings and be blessed in whatever you do in the future.

Or perhaps you thought there are some interesting ideas, and you could lend it to someone else to see what they think. We'll take that as a win, because at least you're not ready to forget about us yet.

Or maybe… Maybe you could tuck this book in your pocket and go walkabout in your local community, visit some of the roads and places less travelled. Start to discover what God is doing, and perhaps join in. Dare to talk to people and get to know them, get excited by their story, do some community stuff, and, who knows, one day launch your own Ignite service.

Naturally, because we are slightly biased, we hope and pray that you will choose option three. And if you do, please drop us a line as we would love to hear how it's all going, as well as having lots of additional material that we would be happy to share.

Finally, as the end draws near, you've probably noticed that we have really enjoyed quoting from various films, books or songs, and so it seems only right to bring you one last quote, which you will find on the next page.

It's a poem, written in the Celtic tradition, from the book *The Edge of Glory* by David Adam, and it manages to encapsulate much that we've been writing about. (Insightful chap, that David.)

*There is a wonderful way to discover God – in the
   other.*
*There is an openness and receptiveness in our lives that
   makes room for the Christ.
   Our mission is not to bring Christ to others, but to
   discover that he is there and reveal his presence.
   When theology palls and mysticism seems empty there is
   still the third way – our neighbour.*
   *'I sought my God,
   My God I could not see.
   I sought my soul,
   My soul eluded me.
   I sought my brother
   And I found all three.'*

Acknowledgements

We would like to thank all those who have enabled Ignite to happen.

Drs Richard and Heather Scott, who sowed the seeds for Ignite through their compassionate care and outreach within the Cliftonville community, and who also supported Ignite in many ways over the ensuing years.

The Revd Hannah Hobday, who was Patrick's curate when Ignite first began in 2007 and worked with him on ideas for the very first Ignite in Cliftonville.

Dawn Evans, who has been a key person on this journey, helping us to write material and deliver Ignite in Cliftonville for many years before going on to set up two Ignites through the Church Commissioners funding in Ashford.

Captain Stuart Budden, from Church Army, who worked with Debbie to test the 'Could Ignite be replicated?' theory and thus was a key person in enabling the first replication of Ignite on the Newington estate in Ramsgate.

Thank you to all those who have been part of the Cliftonville Ignite planning team over the years. Everyone gave valuable input in helping to produce the Ignite material that is now used by many replicated Ignites throughout Canterbury Diocese and on the island of Guernsey.

We would also like to extend our thanks to Canterbury Diocese and the Church Commissioners. They took a risk on a project that looked very different from 'normal' church services, yet they still invested in its outcome.

With us throughout the journey of replication has been the Revd Steve Coneys, the Canterbury diocesan mission and growth advisor, who has worked with us every step of the way to train our team of Ignite mission enablers. His wisdom and his caring, gentle approach have been really appreciated by everyone.

Our thanks also go to the Canterbury Diocese Ignite Board, who have steered us on this journey, especially to Colin Evans, the Revd Jonathan Arnold and Sophia Jones, who actively supported us in writing this book.

Refresh Café is a fun and effective way to build fruitful relationships with parents and carers in your community. It's stay and play turned on its head: the children have fun, but we focus on refreshing the adults with time to talk, fresh coffee, pastries and most importantly our key ingredient: a five-minute 'thought for the day' where we share something of God in a gentle, relevant and accessible way. All this in a welcoming play space for the children. This book shows you how to run Refresh, and includes 33 'thoughts for the day' to use in your setting.

Refresh
Introducing adults to faith through toddler groups
Caroline Montgomery
978 1 80039 216 8 £7.99

brf.org.uk

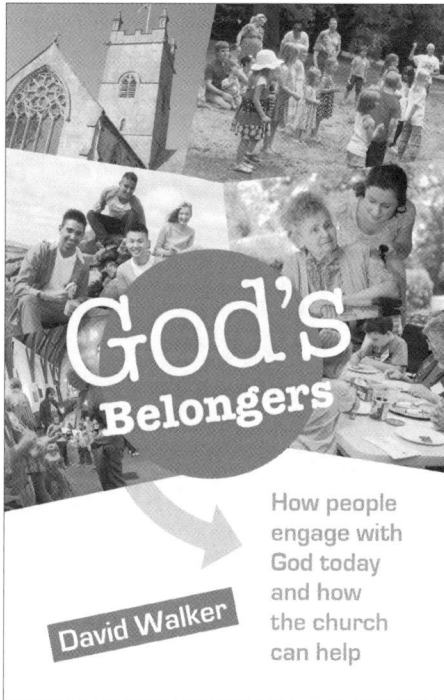

God's
Belongers

How people
engage with
God today
and how
the church
can help

David Walker

This book transforms thinking about church membership by replacing the division between 'members' and 'non-members' with a four-fold model of belonging. Based in extensive practical research, David Walker shows how 'belonging' can encompass a far wider group of people than those who attend weekly services. He examines belonging through relationship, through place and through events, as well as the traditional belonging through activities. He goes on to explore the opportunities for mission that emerge as a result - while also acknowledging the challenges posed for issues such as church financing

God's Belongers
How people engage with God today and how the church can help
David Walker
978 0 85746 467 5 £7.99

brf.org.uk

BRF Ministries

Inspiring people of all ages to grow in Christian faith

BRF Ministries is the
home of Anna Chaplaincy,
Living Faith, Messy Church
and Parenting for Faith

As a charity, our work would not be possible without
fundraising and gifts in wills.
To find out more and to donate,
visit brf.org.uk/give or call +44 (0)1235 462305

Registered with
FUNDRAISING
REGULATOR